D0964214

THE SOULFUL EXPERIENCE

Take Your Company from
So-So to *Soulful*
and Exceed the Expectations of
Your Customers—and Employees

Diane P. Ferraro

WESTBOW
PRESS®
A DIVISION OF THOMAS NELSON
& ZONDERVAN

Copyright © 2018 Diane P. Ferraro.

All rights reserved. No part of this book may be used or reproduced by any means, graphic, electronic, or mechanical, including photocopying, recording, taping or by any information storage retrieval system without the written permission of the author except in the case of brief quotations embodied in critical articles and reviews.

Scriptures taken from the Holy Bible, New International Version®, NIV®. Copyright © 1973, 1978, 1984, 2011 by Biblica, Inc.™ Used by permission of Zondervan. All rights reserved worldwide. www.zondervan.com The "NIV" and "New International Version" are trademarks registered in the United States Patent and Trademark Office by Biblica, Inc.™

This book is a work of non-fiction. Unless otherwise noted, the author and the publisher make no explicit guarantees as to the accuracy of the information contained in this book and in some cases, names of people and places have been altered to protect their privacy.

WestBow Press books may be ordered through booksellers or by contacting:

WestBow Press
A Division of Thomas Nelson & Zondervan
1663 Liberty Drive
Bloomington, IN 47403
www.westbowpress.com
1 (866) 928-1240

Because of the dynamic nature of the Internet, any web addresses or links contained in this book may have changed since publication and may no longer be valid. The views expressed in this work are solely those of the author and do not necessarily reflect the views of the publisher, and the publisher hereby disclaims any responsibility for them.

Any people depicted in stock imagery provided by Getty Images are models, and such images are being used for illustrative purposes only. Certain stock imagery © Getty Images.

ISBN: 978-1-9736-2363-2 (sc)
ISBN: 978-1-9736-2362-5 (e)

Print information available on the last page.

WestBow Press rev. date: 03/23/2018

Soulful: full of or expressing feeling or emotion

Experience: something personally encountered, undergone, or lived through

~ Merriam-Webster

CONTENTS

THE SOULFUL EXPERIENCE

The big business buzzword for the two-thousand teens is "Experience." Glance at agendas for conferences over the past few years and you'll see breakout sessions on "customer experience" or "brand experience" and entire expos and think tanks dedicated solely to the discussion of Experience. User Experience ("UX") is discussed daily at the IT level, but thought leaders at organizations who have been at the forefront of this evolution were part of the UX strategic development early on, and brought in marketing, operations and human resources for a unified approach. It is not a coincidence that these same early-adapter leaders are running the most successful companies in their competitive landscape. Executives who dumped "Experience" into the customer service bucket and gave it no attention after relegating it to the existing customer service team, are now chasing their tails and trying desperately to play catch-up.

The Soulful Experience isn't just the sum of two descriptions from the dictionary. Delivering a Soulful Experience involves a conscientious effort to provide an unforgettable memory to customers. It describes anything from a visit to your website, shopping in your store, using your salon service, dining at your restaurant, staying at your hotel, or even a branded event or party. It can only be accomplished by a cohesive team who genuinely cares about the customer. Companies that consistently get it right with leadership, company culture and giving the customer above and beyond what they expected, deliver The Soulful Experience.

During my time served as marketing director at two of America's largest privately-held jewelers, I was privy to what made one company a Soulful place for customers and employees and the other organization a painful place to work that fought change in most areas, especially when the suggestions came from someone who hadn't "served their time" for at least a year. Most marketing leaders are (or should be) having weekly meetings with the head of operations to find out how well the in-store, restaurant, hotel, amusement park, or web experience is for the customer. Better yet, they should be working the front lines at least monthly to get an accurate pulse of what the customers see, hear, feel, touch and taste. Unfortunately, many CMOs, marketing directors and VPs get stuck in the office (by choice, not by force) and create campaigns and promotions inside a box.

Southwest's founder Herb Kelleher is a legendary leader, not only for starting what is the most financially successful airline in history, but for how he conducted market research. Herb is famous for flying on his planes and sitting in the cabin with all the paying customers. (Anyone who has flown Southwest knows there isn't any segregation with first class, business class and coach cabins.) While in the air, and without revealing his role at the airline, Herb would chat up passengers to find out why they chose to fly Southwest, and what they liked and disliked about the airline and the service. Focus groups and surveys were all fine and dandy, but the one-on-one conversations with the folks are what helped to define the Southwest brand and the Experience that we all know and love (or to use Southwest's spelling – LUV) today.

Some organizations assume that customer experience is no different from Customer Service, but oh, how we have progressed as consumers. Customers who expected average service five years ago have raised the bar, and it isn't enough to have a dedicated toll-free customer service rep to answer calls, nor is an in-store customer service manager going to satisfy the needs of a client. A soulful experience is one where the **entire team** is unified to take care of the customer.

My career of 20-plus years focused on marketing and branding has taught me a great deal about **effective leadership, company culture** and **the customer experience**. Many organizations do an average job in one, maybe two of these areas that contribute to the overall experience. But most fail miserably with at least one, causing the company structure to either crumble or never reach "stretch" goals. Very rarely does a business *excel* in one or two of these areas, and when they do, they develop a loyal legion of fans, both externally with customers and internally with employees and vendors. When an organization nails it on all three fronts, the brand becomes legendary for its outstanding service. After serving in various roles at several small and large corporations since the 1990s, I've recognized that a term was needed to describe this type of rare service. Companies that consistently get it right with leadership, company culture and the customer experience deliver what I call **The Soulful Experience.**

Hooked on Phonics, an educational product that taught children and adults how to read, was my first full-time employer after college. I was hired as a media buyer/director and worked for an entrepreneur who taught me about advertising and running a business, and trusted me with a multimillion dollar budget. He was a generous boss who would surprise us with a delivery of *Legal Seafood* clam chowder, FedExed from Boston to our humble little office in Orange, California. He invited us to use his court-side Lakers tickets, gave anyone who was going on vacation "a little spending cash" (often $200) and personally thanked employees by name for a job well done. Free lunch was also the norm, well before the dotcom boom in Silicon Valley made this a necessity to attract talent. Customers who called the famous toll-free number were also treated well. Each rep was given the authority to donate product based on need, and the thank you cards that came in week after week from grateful mothers, fathers, grandparents and teachers was heartwarming.

The company was known for its stellar customer service and word-of-mouth referrals long before Yelp, Facebook and Twitter. Although it was a direct response company and helped customers via a toll-free number (if you're over 30 you probably have 1-800-ABCDEFG embedded in your brain, thanks to the infomercials we ran 24/7 on national and local cable TV), the experience was superb as agents were empowered to talk with callers as long as needed, and they were allowed to go "off-script" to make sure the service was personal.

This was several years prior to Tony Hsieh starting Zappos and the legendary call center that delivers happiness.

After five years I moved to a Japanese-based original equipment manufacturer with global operations for a start-up division in the cellular and navigation industries. What a wake-up call that was, being one of over 100,000 employees after coming from a small family-owned business with a staff of only 200. The company was B2B (business to business), and the culture was at the opposite end of the spectrum from Hooked on Phonics. One vivid example of "us and them" was at a lavish holiday party thrown for three Southern California divisions and key executives from company headquarters, with approximately 2,000 employees and their guests in attendance. The executives were called to the buffet at 7:00 pm. My table, which included the engineers and a few marketers from the Carlsbad office, weren't invited to get our food until close to 9:00 pm, long after the executives had finished dessert and coffee. Our industrial engineer joked that we could have had pizza delivered to our table and finished and still have been hungry by the time we went up to the buffet.

Eventually, I found my way back to another family-run business, this time run by a dynamic young husband and wife team who started 1-800-WEDDING out of their garage when they were just 19 years old. Their mission was to help couples plan the wedding of their dreams using the website and call-center that provided prescreened vendors that fit within the bride's budget. Up to this point, before TheKnot and MyWedding.com, brides had to pour through wedding magazines and phone books to contact dress shops, reception sites, florists, caterers, DJs, bakers and photographers. Donne and Cindy Kerestic's tech savvy and personal experience in the wedding industry were a hit with couples and vendors in Southern California, and they were ready to expand to other major markets. They wanted someone with national media planning, direct response, public relations and general marketing experience, and as soon as I met them and was offered a position to lead the team, I couldn't wait to start.

Donne eventually took his idea to one of the top privately owned jewelry chains in the country (you'll read more about this later) and shortly following the dotcom bust in 2000, I went along to join him at another family-run business. Today, Donne and his wife run *Chapel of the Flowers* in Las Vegas, a hugely successful and very elegant one-acre wedding venue with unique indoor and outdoor chapels.

After learning from some of the best leaders in business (and also taking notes on what to *never do* from folks with executive titles, but not the leadership or people skills that make a true leader) I've come up with five simple steps on how to deliver The Soulful Experience.

Some of you reading this may feel that the steps are no brainers. Other readers might wonder why you aren't already doing these things. If you're a busy CEO who is traveling all the time, you might be thinking about emailing your VP of HR or a trusted manager to ask if your company is executing any of the five steps on the list. This book is intended for start-up, small and mid-sized organizations who haven't had the budget to bring in strategists, brand experts and marketing consultants. My hope is that any company that isn't getting top marks internally from employees, or with paying customers, will read it and implement at least some of the ideas.

"There is nothing more important to our business than bringing an unforgettable experience to our customers. Our commitment to providing a memorable experience has built our small business into a worldwide brand. Each year, over 5,000 couples from 50+ different countries put their trust in us to deliver a memorable event that will be remembered for a lifetime."

Donne Kerestic, CEO
Chapel of the Flowers, Las Vegas

GET THE CURRENT PULSE OF YOUR BRAND EXPERIENCE

If you've been to Disneyland as an adult, you've likely noticed how everything (other than the crowds and exorbitant ticket prices) is absolutely perfect. Friendly greeters welcome you at the entrance, just before you spot the hillside Disneyland logo created in seasonal flowers, the iconic clock at the train station towering above. The smell of buttered popcorn and cotton candy wafting out of the Main Street shops beckoning taste buds to indulge in something savory or sweet, even at 9am. Mickey Mouse, Goofy, Snow White and Buzz Lightyear delight visitors, pose for photos and sign autograph books. And then, in the distance, you see it: Sleeping Beauty's Castle, one of the most photographed attractions in the entire world.

Every sense is tantalized at the Magic Kingdom, a man-made wonderland in the suburbs, built on a former orange grove.

Walt Disney had a distinct vision of what his amusement park would be to visitors: a place that upheld American values and where parents and children could enjoy time together. He even referred to it as a "physical experience." The day of the Anaheim, California grand opening in 1955, Walt Disney stated that "Disneyland is dedicated to the ideals, the dreams, and the hard facts that have created America." (Smithsonian.com) This park wasn't going to be about rides and carnival games. This park represented the American Dream and would give visitors a chance to escape reality for one day. The genius of Walt Disney was not only his creative talent, but his understanding of human psychology. The inherent need of people young and old to make an emotional connection to each other, and to brands and products. Disneyland would eventually be known as "The Happiest Place on Earth," a tagline first used in 1972, and quite a testament to its namesake and visionary.

You may not be a theme park CEO. You might own a few pizzerias and are struggling to compete with $5.99 offers from national chains, or run a local coffee shop and are worried about losing market share to the "green lady" who is moving in across the street. Maybe your family has a well-respected regional jewelry store chain and not sure how to compete with the online players, or the auto dealership you run isn't getting as much advertising support from your corporate parent as the other manufacturers provide. You recognize a need to connect with your customers (Walt Disney called them *guests*) on an emotional level but aren't sure where or how to start. Great customer service is considered the norm today, and anyone entering your establishment or visiting your website must feel that they are not just purchasing a commodity or basic service. Customers must "feel" that something different is taking place, a unique experience unlike anything they've seen in your town, your industry, or at your competitor down the street.

Soulful Experience Tip:

Change the rules and create a new sub-industry within your industry.

When I was in college back in the late 1980s, I got hooked on coffee. I'd drink it morning, noon and night. I loved the taste - and buzz - so much, that I'd even skip meals and fill up on the hot beverage every season except summer. If I didn't feel like brewing a pot at our apartment, I'd stop by the 7-Eleven that was on my walk home from the UNLV campus and pick up a fresh cup of coffee, with a few of the delicious flavored creamers, for under a dollar. This was a gourmet treat at a time when I was making around $4 an hour working part-time at Saks Fifth Avenue, when I only knew Starbuck as a character in Moby Dick, long before I heard of baristas serving venti espresso drinks for astronomical prices.

A decent cup of coffee could be had at any donut shop or Denny's, and to my knowledge, no one had been complaining that it was *just so difficult* to find a place that sold expensive gourmet coffee. But what two business partners realized - and Starbucks' guru Howard Schulz implemented after visiting Italy and seeing how espresso cafes brought people together - was that what Americans *needed* was a local community gathering place where a dark roasted coffee would be served. Starbucks took an ordinary, inexpensive beverage that Americans took for granted, built comfortable and hip "living rooms" on street corners across the country, and made meeting for coffee an experience that is part of our cultural landscape today.

Robbins Brothers, The Engagement Ring Store, did something remarkable, but on a much smaller scale. When brothers Steve and Skip managed their family's chain of popular William Pitt jewelry stores in Southern California malls, they discovered they had an identity problem when a customer asked what store he was in when writing a check to pay for a gift. William Pitt was well known in the region, but to shoppers they were just another jewelry store in a sea of jewelry stores in the mall. After studying the competitive landscape, analyzing top selling items in recent years, and asking themselves what type of company they wanted to run in the future, they decided that their strategy would be to focus the business on bridal jewelry: engagement rings, diamonds and wedding bands.

While other mall jewelers were paying experienced salespeople to change watch batteries, pierce ears, sell inexpensive silver and the occasional diamond necklace or engagement ring, Steve and Skip closed their mall stores and started moving bridal inventory to former bank buildings in neighborhoods where people drove by daily between work and home. The name changed to Robbins Brothers, The World's Biggest Engagement Ring Store, and each location had up to 10,000 square feet of retail space with case after case of sparkling diamond engagement rings, wedding bands for men and women, and just a few cases of diamond stud earrings, pendants, pearls and other jewelry gifts perfect for the wedding day and anniversaries. Changing the business strategy helped everything else fall into place, from marketing to hiring to acquiring real estate for new locations.

Advertising copywriters now had clear direction of who the audience was they needed to target, and the media buyers knew exactly what demographics they needed to reach. The "help wanted" ads touted the unique business strategy too, with the staid description for "jewelry salespeople" replaced with a creative post that asked for applicants who desired to help couples find a once-in-a-lifetime purchase that would be the symbol of their love. (One memorable job posting had the headline "Do you like to make people cry?" and went on to explain that when couples get engaged, they cry tears of joy.)

Skip and Steve took a business that had been commodity-based and turned it into one of the most successful experience-driven destination stores in the country. Couples came from up to 50 miles away to see what the World's Biggest Engagement Ring Store offered, and often spent four or five hours trying on rings, learning about diamonds - and ultimately making a purchase.

Soulful Experience Tip:

Focus on creating a unique, memorable experience that will ensure your brand stands out and gives customers a reason to do business with you.

Many companies get a few things right when it comes to experience, but organizations that put the customers – and employees – at the heart of the brand gain a stellar reputation and win market share from the competition. These examples of recent Soulful Experiences are worth reading, and then sharing with your team to inspire change within your organization.

Southwest Airlines

I travel frequently to Southern California and Las Vegas for work and to check in on my father who now resides in a terrific assisted living facility. Airfare to Orange County and Las Vegas can be found for as low as $49 during price wars, and I've flown the skies with just about every airline that departs from Denver.

Most of the time I travel light, carrying a small suitcase that is placed in the overhead bin. But these days several airlines charge a fee even for carryon luggage. If you don't plan ahead and prepay for this "benefit" you could double the cost of your ticket if you pay at the counter. Traveling is stressful enough, and who wants to pay more for simply taking the necessities with you on a business trip, or a vacation for that matter? And I don't need to go into the stories of passengers being bumped or forcibly removed from flights, stranded in airports, stuck on the tarmac in an uncomfortably warm or cold plane for hours, or standing in a long line (due to understaffed counters) to check luggage, only to be told when they get to the front that they missed the check-in time and will therefore miss their flight, without any compensation.

Southwest Airlines, co-founded by Herb Kelleher and under the leadership of CEO Gary Kelly since 2008, is abnormal not just in the aviation industry but in the world of business. Every employee is asked to live "the Southwest Way," which is to have a Servant's Heart, a Fun-LUVing Attitude, and a Warrior Spirit. The employees really do practice what the handbook preaches, as I've been on several trips where the flight attendants sing, celebrate customers' birthdays and anniversaries, and the pilots still invite the kids to see the cockpit. You never lose money or pay a penalty when cancelling or changing a flight ahead of time, as you are provided with a credit to use towards another flight within 12 months.

Added bonus: they allow you to check two bags for free AND you get to bring carryon luggage at no charge. This low-cost airline is one of the most profitable on Wall Street, and it doesn't appear anyone else is close to catching up with them.

Something else that Southwest inherently understands and that is going to be tough to replicate is their hyper-focus on taking care of the customer. My hunch is hiring people who agree to live "the Southwest Way" is 90% of the reason this company is successful year after year, and why customers are fiercely loyal to the brand. Having a Servant's Heart might seem easy when you're on the clock and you're getting paid to help passengers find their way to gates, clean up spilled drinks or find a way for a parent and child to sit together on a plane that has only single open seats in the very front and very back. But going above and beyond is second-nature to Southwest employees, and as I write this section I've just been alerted to this trending story on Twitter:

"Southwest Airlines Employee Personally Delivers Luggage to Cancer Patient's Home."

People, by Jason Duaine Hahn, August 11, 2017

The tweet links to a story on People.com, and shows a photo of two lovely women, all smiles, one holding a bouquet of roses, standing in front of a Southwest counter. My initial thought is "Outstanding work by the PR team!"

As I read the story, my heartstrings are pulled. The passenger, Stacy Hurt, was flying to Pittsburgh from Nashville for chemotherapy treatment the next morning. Her original flight was rerouted and cancelled and her luggage was stuck in Nashville. The contents: medication that helped with chemo side effects, and of equal importance were the precious rosary and lucky t-shirt that helped with the emotional side effects of the cancer treatment she would undergo for hours.

Sarah Rowan, the customer service agent who received the phone call late in the evening, wasn't *told* she had to do anything. Normal protocol was to have a courier deliver the suitcase to the passenger the next day. But anyone with a Servant's Heart would know that this wasn't a normal situation. And when the luggage came in on the last flight, after 1:30 am and after the couriers were gone, the customer service agent (who by the way, is only 27, for any naysayers who assume millennials don't want to work hard or go the extra mile) looked up the passenger's address and, after her shift ended, drove 25 minutes to personally deliver the luggage to Stacy's home. Arrival time: 3:30. In the *morning*.

Stacy awoke to find her suitcase on the porch, and was grateful for the courier who dropped it off. Upon opening the suitcase she found this note:

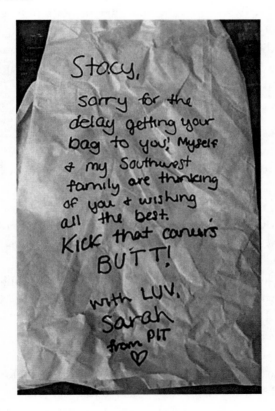

When was the last time someone at your company went out of their way, after clocking out, to do something remarkable for a customer?

Southwest Airlines is known for these types of stories that are shared on social networks on a daily basis. Very rarely does the story get covered by People.com, but they aren't in it for the free publicity. They walk the walk, and provide a Soulful Experience in an industry that is, unfortunately, known for consistently delivering *below average* customer service.

The Southwest Way is also defined by providing grants to help people create and sustain public places in communities, surprising travelers with free concerts on flights and in terminals, and featuring the vibrant artwork of young hospital patients on the normally vanilla-white bulkheads.

Oh, I thought it was also worth mentioning this company with a quaint view on loving the customer and treating their employees well is worth $20.4 billion. (2016 earnings)

Chik-fil-A

Miss Ruby, a youthful 91-year-old, visits Chick-fil-A in Waxahachie, Texas to play bingo. The local marketing director hosts the game every Thursday and the players consist of mostly sharp elderly folks who live in the community. She made a friend with eight-year-old Brenden, a little fellow who met Miss Ruby and asked if he could join in on the game.

The fast-food chicken restaurant, as famous for being closed on Sundays as they are for waffle fries, is not your typical drive-thru chain. (And I promise I'm not playing favorites because I'm addicted to the frosted lemonade.)

When you wait in the drive-thru on a typical weekday, there are at least 20 cars ahead of you. "Am I going to be in line for my entire lunch break?" your inner voice asks. "Good question," you answer to no one. But within a minute or two, if the weather is good, you'll be greeted by a friendly employee who walks up to your car, offers to show you a menu, and takes your order. Before you know it, you're at the pick-up window, handing over your cash or credit card, and soon your car smells of tasty fried chicken and yes, those sinful waffle fries.

Chick-fil-A is just one of 50,000 fast food chains in the United States, and when you combine hunger with hurried, you'll pull into just about any parking lot. So why does this chicken chain see annual sales of over $3.5 million per restaurant and total company revenue of $7 billion (Nation's Restaurant News, June 2017) compared with $2.5 million on average for McDonald's and over three times more than KFC, with $1 million per restaurant?

Founder Truett Cathy established clear biblical principles early on for his company, with the vision "To glorify God by being a faithful steward of all that is entrusted to us and to have a positive influence on all who come into contact with Chick-fil-A." This was the filter that everything ran through, and is undoubtedly the singular reason for the organization's success. Hiring the right people at every level who embrace being a "faithful steward" and knowing what it is to be a "servant leader" enables the company to provide a service to customers that far exceeds what they get at other national chains.

Dee Ann Turner, Vice President, Enterprise Social Responsibility at Chick-fil-A, authored the book *It's My Pleasure: The Impact of Extraordinary Talent and Compelling Culture* and sums up the secret sauce of the organization's culture:

- Recruit for Success: the talent selection process focuses on three C's: character, competency and chemistry.
- Nurture Talent by Telling the Truth: Being honest with employees creates a culture of trust and results in loyalty.
- Engage Guests in Your Culture: regardless of the location, the Chick-fil-A guest (customer) is treated with honor, dignity, and respect.

Customers are also brand ambassadors at Chick-fil-A. Chances are you'll see someone – or an entire family - wearing a cow costume on a Saturday. If one person in the office mentions he's heading to Chick-fil-A for lunch, there will be more than a carful of coworkers wanting to join him. The brand is also famous for their "new restaurant camp-outs" where the first 100 people in line will win free Chick-Fil-A for an entire year. Hey, a chicken sandwich meal, complete with waffle fries and a medium drink, is nearly six bucks, which adds up to $312 of free lunch for 52 weeks. That's over $31,000 in free meals the fast food restaurant gives away before they even open for business.

Pier-1 Imports

This might seem like an odd choice, especially when the home goods category is so competitive with online and offline retailers. The catchy commercials during the holidays show that this store has unexpected offerings, but when a woman hears voices from a nutcracker or pillow, my guess is that someone was doing a little post-happy hour shopping.

Why I chose Pier-1 Imports as a company that delivered a Soulful Experience is three-fold:

1. The online shopping was easy and the price was right;
2. The product I decided not to keep (four patio chairs) could be returned in the local store;
3. When I arrived at the store, the staff went out of their way to help me.

The day I drove to the store to return the chairs was also the day the strip mall's property manager was repaving half of the parking lot. There were so many cars waiting for a space to open up that one may have thought it was Christmas Eve. Navigating the narrow makeshift lanes was challenging in my SUV, but I finally found a spot between two cones and uncomfortably close to Hooters at lunchtime. It was the farthest spot from Pier-1 but I figured I'd get my steps in for the day with a few trips to carry the chairs inside.

No sooner than I pulled the first chair out of the back than a young man with an apron was running towards me yelling "I'm here to help!" I looked around to see who he was calling out to, then realized it was me. Not an elderly person, nor an attractive young lady, just your average middle-aged woman, with four red patio chairs in the back of the SUV.

This young employee, about 20 years old, had a furniture dolly and was at my car in under a minute. I must have looked surprised, as he apologized for startling me. He then proceeded to apologize for the parking lot mess, and said he was glad I decided to make the effort to visit their store. I told him I was only returning items I purchased online and he thanked me for coming in.

The manager was there holding the door open, walked me to the register, and naturally asked me if I wanted to exchange the chairs for anything else. When I declined and said I just wanted to return them and get the credit back on my Visa, he didn't push or prod and instead thanked me for coming in, completed the transaction, and invited me back to the store to shop when I had more time. I was in and out of the store in five minutes, and was actually smiling.

This was a splendid example of a Soulful Experience. I'm not sure if other Pier 1 Imports operate on the same level, but it doesn't really matter to me. All that I care about is the local store cares about me as an individual and they went out of their way to make sure I had a positive experience when I was making a RETURN. You bet I will be heading back to that specific store (near Park Meadows Mall, a suburb of Denver) the next time I need new pillows, candles or other items for my home.

The Necessary Deep-Dive into Your Current State of the Company

Before you can perform brand surgery, you need to know the vital signs. As CEO, you're the chief surgeon of your organization. Perhaps there's a major emergency and you need to take action immediately or you're looking at options for an elective procedure. Prior to making any changes to personnel, procedures or product offerings, make sure you know where your company is positioned. Here are ways to get the current pulse of your brand:

**Monthly sales volume, customer traffic
and trends for past three years**
(or since inception if your company has been
in business less than three years)

- Review with your CFO or head of finance to highlight periods of growth and decline
- Any seasonality or calendar changes that are not the norm (i.e. winter storm/power outage, February 1 - 5, 2017)
- Note what attributed to these periods. Were factors external - local economy boom or bust, positive or negative news, election, etc.? Or internal - new hire costs, taxes, insurance premiums?
- Overlap with marketing and sales calendar to find correlations with campaigns, promotions, public relations/media stories, changes with local competition
- If you haven't been reviewing year-over-year sales with your executive team at least once a month (ideally weekly), start doing this immediately

Business Plan, Marketing Strategy, and Goals by Department

- Meet with your executive team and all department heads to review your current business plan. When was it last updated?
- Does it address what is going on nationally, locally and economically? Has the marketing strategy evolved with your customers and competition?
- Does each department head have clear goals that support the overall business plan?

Competitive Landscape

- If you're in an industry where competitors are part of a publicly traded company, you can find detailed information with some in-depth Google searching
- Hire secret shoppers to visit the competition (if a physical location exists) and provide them with a clear list of items to research
- Check with advertising websites to see if they publish a list of top advertisers by market in your industry. You'll see the "rate card" spend here and can assume that the real number is about 15-20% less than reported.
- Review industry trade publications for up-to-date information on the major players. If you don't see anything about the competitive landscape (top 100 lists, highest dollar billings for year prior), contact the editor and see if they have any reports available for purchase. Greenbook.org lists research firms by industry and region. If you can allocate funds for hiring an independent firm or consultant, be clear about the return on investment and contact references they've worked with in recent months before you sign a contract.

Customer Reviews

- Meet with your customer service/experience manager and go over customer reviews from past three years.
- Note any changes in sentiment, comments/ratings by location, and overall brand reputation. What is the turnaround time to respond to customer complaints?
- Have complaints increased or decreased?
- What top 10 issues received the most complaints?
- Look at the facts and address what needs be done with the key players.

- Create a spreadsheet or subscribe to a software service like Hootsuite that alerts you whenever your brand name is mentioned in a review.
- Subscribe to Google Alerts.
- Monitor brand mentions on your social channels several times a day (Facebook, Twitter, Pinterest, Snapchat, Instagram) and check Yelp, Better Business Bureau and other review sites.

Note: If you don't have a dedicated customer experience team, assign this responsibility to one of your executives or managers as soon as possible.

Employee Sentiment and Retention

- Human Resources should have exit interviews from employees who voluntarily leave the company. Read through these and set aside any that indicate culture problems within a team or the company as a whole.
- Consider implementing anonymous "stay interviews" for employees to voluntarily complete annually. This will give you insight as to why good employees decide to stay at your company, and you'll likely have constructive criticism as well. (Learning from long-term team members may provide more important and relevant feedback than you'll receive from customers.)
- Review Glassdoor, Great Place to Work, Indeed and other local sites that share anonymous employee reviews and ratings on companies. (Also do a Google search of your company name to see if there are any blog posts or stories about your workplace.)

If your organization does business with several outside vendors, consider creating a survey that allows them to anonymously answer questions about the team they work with, satisfaction with billing and payables, and level of professionalism on phone, via email, and when meeting in the office.

One of the best examples of a leader knowing the sentiment of his team was Jesus. In Luke 5 we see Jesus teaching a crowd on the shore of the Sea of Galilee. Nearby, fishermen were washing their nets, discouraged after a long night of hard work and without catching anything. (1-5.) I can certainly relate to the fishermen, as I'm sure anyone who has been in business for more than a year can, too. No fish meant that there was nothing to be sold at market the next day, and they felt unbearable pressure. Jesus knew they were desperate and calmly instructed the men to go out to deep water, and drop the nets again. (Verse 4.) When they caught so many fish the nets began to break and they had to call for another boat to come help, they trusted this Man who took them in a new direction and taught them not to give up.

As a leader, do you know your team well enough to sense when someone is discouraged? When was the last time you took an individual aside, asked what was going on, and then offered advice to help her or him succeed?

I had a boss once who told me I needed to be tougher, that I was too nice to be a leader. The words hit me hard, as I was trying unsuccessfully to get into management, but being "mean" just wasn't part of my DNA. (Not that I was always nice. Just ask those closest to me who felt the brunt of a rare bad mood.) That advice however did turn into an ah-a moment, as it encouraged me to do some soul-searching and figure out exactly what type of boss I wanted to be. I worked on my confidence and decided that I was going to be the boss who listens, who mentors, and who helps team members fulfill their career and personal dreams. I can't take credit for the success of people who I've worked with or manage, but I do feel I know how to spot and nurture talent.

Richard Branson started his career at age 15, a poor high school dropout. Today he is a billionaire, owns more than 400 companies within the Virgin Group (Virgin America, Virgin Atlantic, Virgin Mobile, Virgin Records), and is the founder of the first commercial "spaceline" with plans to democratize space.

Famous for not only taking huge risks, he has an inherent understanding of employee morale and customer experience. Sir Branson spends approximately 25% of his time doing publicity stunts and marketing for his companies, supporting the teams by being present at the offices, openings and events. Training programs are far from the norm, as employees learn how to salsa dance and change tires on race cars.

> *"Clients do not come first. Employees come first. If you take care of your employees, they will take care of the clients."*
> **–Sir Richard Branson**

This is a billionaire who still maintains meaningful contact with his teams, and no doubt because of his focus on communication with employees, Sir Richard Branson's portfolio continues to grow with successful and profitable companies.

Where to Start

An outstanding customer service experience is expected. Gone are the days when a client of a tire shop or a fast-food restaurant went in only for the special deal and didn't complain if they were treated poorly or if the restroom was a mess. Social media has empowered everyone who has buying power, from a child spending his allowance on candy at the mall, to a teenager purchasing a movie ticket with hard-earned cash from babysitting, to the senior citizen getting her hair colored and styled at the beauty salon.

Small business owners, and to some extent executives who have been in the workforce for 20+ years, know the value of social media, but may not realize that the "voice of the customer" is SHOUTED on the internet, oftentimes unbeknownst to the brand. That is, until the comment is shared with others in the customer's social circles and possibly even goes viral. A company that has a stellar online reputation will likely have other customers weigh in on a comment, and if the comment is negative, brand loyalists will jump in and defend the company. And if the company has a strong overall rating, one bad review from a random unhappy customer needn't cause undue panic. The post could possibly be from an unethical competitor, too. What is vital is that a company representative join in the conversation, address the situation, and if the post is negative, take the conversation offline and literally "off the page" as soon as possible.

First impressions when searching the web can make or break a customer's decision to visit your establishment. Below are screenshots for two restaurant searches in the Newport Beach/Costa Mesa area in Orange County, California:

I've been to Rothchild's and can assure you that it is one of the finest restaurants in coastal Orange County. You'll receive the impeccable service one would expect when spending $50 or more for an entrée, the cuisine is decadent, and the interior that is featured in the Google listing represents the upscale, traditional decor.

However, La Cave has comparable ratings, and their decision to feature a photo of an elegant surf and turf meal will likely be attractive to foodies.

The manager or employee responsible for social media and brand reputation at each restaurant would be wise to review the photos and revise frequently to ensure new online visitors are seeing seasonal offerings and more attractive interior and exterior views. Rothschild's in particular should work on increasing the total number of Google reviews as they may be losing new patrons who are in town on business or vacation.

Here's what you need to do today: block out 60 minutes and Google your company name and cities where you have locations. Take screen shots of your reviews and then compare with searches for your top three competitors. Next, go to the "images" tab at top and see what photos are listed on page one. Do you see photos that best represent your brand? How many photos are generated by your team and how many were posted by fans, brand ambassadors, bloggers and employees?

List everything you love, like and hate, and set up time to meet with your executive team to share the results. And let the team know to be ready to meet soon to discuss strategy.

Field Trip

Now that you've got a taste of your company's reputation, it's time for a "customer experience journey" field trip.

A magnificent business consultant once took senior management at a company I worked for on what I call a "retail safari." We were grouped into teams of five and each team had a checklist that included the first impression of the store, the staff's attentiveness, displays and inventory. I encourage you to take your leadership team on this "safari" and adapt it to your industry. If you're a restaurant or bar owner, visit other service industries, including hotels. If you run brake and oil change stations and want to reach more women, consider checking out salons, spas and boutiques where women frequent. Take the journey within and outside your industry, with the ultimate goal of educating the leadership team on how other businesses treat customers.

Appoint a "leadership coach" to manage the safari, break out the teams, draft the checklist and do follow-up. The coach will assign three locations for each team to visit, and upon completion, the teams will meet as a group and discuss their findings.

The group will then vote on the "best" and the "worst" customer journey and apply what was learned to the company's own customer experience and incorporate the notes into the strategy, training, products and service.

Customer Experience Journey Checklist:

Each team member will use this checklist and provide comments for each section.

Store/Restaurant/Brand: _____ Location: _____

- Before you go into the location, discuss what you already know about the brand
- First impressions: the greeting, the smell, the sounds, the appearance of the entryway
- Displays: well-stocked, clean/dust-free, easy to understand
- Pretend the store has no signage: would you know where you're at, and what the brand stands for? Does the merchandising, staff, colors, etc. fit the brand perception?
- The staff: how were you treated? was the experience pushy? Is there any reason you'd buy in-store versus shopping online or elsewhere?
- Follow-up after the visit

What does this company do best that we should incorporate into our strategy and experience?

What does this company do poorly that we should make sure we never do?

Would you shop at this store again, or tell friends about it, based on your experience?

THE SOULFUL EXPERIENCE ASSESSMENT

Does **your** business provide a Soulful customer experience, or is improvement needed?

Take this quick Soulful Experience assessment:

Rate Your Experience on a Scale of 1-7
(1 – oh-no/poor experience, 7 - "The Soulful Experience")

Initial perception of brand   _____
(Website/digital ad, other advertising, reputation)

Exterior appearance & signage   _____
(Window displays, parking lot, sidewalk in front of place)

Greeting once inside   _____
(How long did it take to be acknowledged?)

Appearance of establishment once inside   _____

That extra "something" (beverage, snacks, live musician?)   _____

Cleanliness of main area, restrooms, counters, checkout   _____

Quality of product and service
(Whether socks or sake, candy or chicken cordon bleu)   _____

Employee expertise, confidence and attentiveness   _____

Do you want to be part of this brand's story?   _____

Point of sale   _____
(Wait time, explanation of return policy, warranty, etc.)

Follow-up after the sale   _____
(i.e. personal phone call or email, thank you card)

                                                   Total: _____

Score of 70-77:	Soulful Experience
Score of 55-69:	So-so Experience
Score of less than 55:	Oh-no Experience

If you scored in the Soulful Experience range, congrats! Send an email to me at <u>diane@thesoulfulexperience.com</u> and I'll send you a digital badge to place on your website and social pages that will let the world know you provide a Soulful Experience.

Didn't come close to getting 56 points? Don't worry, keep reading and soon you'll have everything you need to raise your score. The assessment is provided again at the end of the book.

CREATE A SOULFUL STRATEGY

In-house marketers tend to put blinders on when it comes to campaigns outside their own industry. Early on in my career this was my albatross, but thanks to wise business leaders in my midst I learned to be open-minded and observant, and started to seek out innovative ads and ways of selling in areas outside my zone.

I was exposed to a new type of customer experience in 2006, and it started with an introduction to the owners of Kleinfeld. I traveled to New York to visit a bridal gown store, but not to see the latest trends in wedding dresses. Our mission: to meet Mara Urshel and Ronnie Rothstein, who along with Wayne Rogers (of M.A.S.H. fame) purchased Kleinfeld from venture capitalists and expanded it into the most famous wedding dress store in the world. Even before the reality show "Say Yes to the Dress" made Kleinfeld a household name and turned the employees into reality stars, brides with above-average budgets made this store with 400 dresses the first stop after getting engaged.

Prior to Kleinfeld, Mara Urshel was already a legend in the retail world. She was senior vice president and GMM at Saks Fifth Avenue and an executive with Geoffrey Beene and Casual Corner. Her eye for style and quality is credited to contributing to the launch of Isaac Mizrahi and Michael Kors. And while luxury apparel, trendspotting and relationships with manufacturers were keys to Mara's success, her proven ability to connect with customers is what sets her apart.

Kleinfeld first opened in 1941 with a store in Brooklyn that offered special occasion dresses and fur coats. It wasn't until 1968 when co-owner and family member Hedda Kleinfeld started offering designer wedding gowns from Europe. Then in 1979, the store did away with furs and eveningwear and focused on bridal only. The family sold the store to a group of VCs in 1990, who then sold the store to another group of VCs in 1996.

A bridal store with a long history of catering to the east coast elite wasn't doing anything wrong. They didn't necessarily need to do anything else to retain bridal market share. But when Kleinfeld came up for sale in 1999, Mara, Ronnie and Wayne knew that there was more in that store than expensive wedding gowns, veils and accessories. There was a Customer Experience ready to be unveiled, something until then the world had not yet seen.

Brides would make appointments and travel to the Brooklyn store by limousine with their mothers and friends to find the one dress from over 800 styles that Kleinfeld now carried. The excitement of shopping for the perfect dress was highlighted with champagne and personal attendants who patiently pulled style after style until the bride and her guests were all in agreement. Mara and Ronnie were delivering a high level of retail service, but they knew that if they opened a store in Manhattan, they'd be able to expand the showroom and offer even more brides-to-be the chance to shop like a princess.

In 2005, the beautiful bridal destination opened in Manhattan. A 35,000 square feet boutique with 1,500 designer dresses to try on, 28 dressing rooms and a staff of 250 employees. It wasn't long after this opening that my team member Tracey Lyles and I toured Kleinfeld with Mara as our gracious guide, introducing us to the staff, letting us share in the joy of brides standing on the pedestal and modeling their gowns, and watching tears roll down the faces of proud mothers. It was an experience unlike anything I'd ever seen.

No pressure. No rushing. No judging. No hard-selling.

The lobby and showroom were incredible, and room after room of gorgeous silk, lace and taffeta gowns were the dresses of fairytales. But what I remember most about my visit with Mara that day was what went on behind the scenes. The efficiency of the electric rolling racks in the back, quickly transporting dresses to the front of the store where personal shoppers would find the styles within their client's budget. The rolling racks also moved the custom designs, handmade to fit a bride's exact proportions, to the seamstresses, who would check to ensure everything was correct before contacting the bride to come in for the fitting.

Every employee was excited to be working at Kleinfeld. Mara addressed each team member by name, and asked specific questions that pertained to the department. It was obvious that Mara cared about the company culture at Kleinfeld. Employees had a purpose and each step was intentional. The pace was fast and each employee had to think quick and make rapid-fire decisions to not only meet the expectations of the friends and family helping the bride, but most importantly to find *The Dress*. It isn't often you find employees working retail with smiles on their faces as they work frenetically, standing or walking for an entire shift. But Kleinfeld isn't retail. It is more like a hospitality or service business that just happens to sell designer wedding gowns, and unlike a typical store, Kleinfeld provides a Soulful Experience that brides will never forget.

Chances are you've been part of a family-owned or start-up organization that was guilty of going full-speed ahead with the excitement of a new venture, anxious to sell products or provide a service, without having a strategic plan. Many companies have been guilty of lacking strategy, and some have been quite successful, up to a point. Then when a new player enters the market or industry and disrupts the status quo, sales start to decline and employee morale goes out the window. Without a strategic plan, a once thriving company suddenly unravels. Oftentimes a company with good intentions will a have a business plan and sales goals, but not work through the current and projected scenarios in their industry. If you want your business to not just succeed, but thrive, it is vital to have a strategy in place that looks out at the horizon for the next five years.

If you're opening a new business and don't yet have a strategic plan, set up a meeting with your key team players and partners before you do anything else. It is imperative that the owner or president take on this responsibility. Assign certain aspects, such as managing the timeline and completion date to vice presidents or directors, but ultimately it is the head of the company who needs to show the entire organization that the strategic plan is your top priority. Taking ownership of the strategy also sends the message that you're "all-in" and that you care about every aspect of the business.

Soulful Experience Tip:

**Start breaking down silos with a
business strategy that requires
the ownership of every team member.**

Having a well thought out strategy is essential during times of war and peace, which could describe any business, right? There isn't anything mysterious about thinking strategically or writing up a strategy that is soulful. It is simply a way to look at your company and thoughtfully include details about what makes your brand soulful. This is an opportunity to document how you stand out in your industry, to recognize your company's strengths, weaknesses, opportunities and threats (SWOT), and establish clearly defined goals for each division of your organization: operations, sales, customer service, marketing, IT, manufacturing or merchandising, personnel, real estate, facilities, etc.

Carter McNamara, MBA/PhD and author of the blog www. managementhelp.org states on his website that the process of planning is in some ways more important than the end result. His section on strategic planning is filled with resources and examples that would benefit any company in early growth stages. Strategic planning is essential for any organization and it is more than a mere document that the team refers to during meetings. A company that works together to develop a strategy is breaking down silos between departments, and gives each leader insight into what the other departments need to do to hit the strategic goals.

Before you get started on your strategy, first know what your brand wants to be as it matures. Your dreams, and the details to make your dreams come true, also known as Vision and Mission, are quick snapshots of your company to current and future employees. Well written vision and mission statements help those inside and outside your organization understand what you do and why you do it. Customers and vendors will also look to your vision and mission statements as a way to size your brand up against others in the industry and community and know what makes you better, different, and trustworthy.

VISION and MISSION

Writing your vision and mission statements doesn't require an MBA, but isn't a cake walk either. This is serious business. The vision isn't just a poetic statement you engrave and put up on a wall in the lobby. The mission statement shouldn't be relegated to the employee handbook, only to be forgotten after the first week of work.

The vision and mission should become an organic part of your organization. Some companies require that staff members memorize the statements, but even more crucial is to have a vision and mission that is "felt" and absorbed, something that describes what the company stands for and is referred to by every level of employee for every task performed. Employees wouldn't need to recite the these verbatim but should know, without a doubt, what the brand represents with key words and phrases that easily convey the Big Dream and the Details that make that dream happen.

If you need some inspiration, take a cue from a few organizations and brands you may recognize…

The United Nations

The U.N. has a letter written by Danilo Turk with a section simply titled

Vision Statement: People First

The subsequent paragraph opens with

> *"My vision for the United Nations begins with the world's peoples and the duty of the Organization to address their needs fairly and effectively."*

Companies with a clear vision that resonates with a specific target audience are known for having loyal customers who are fans and fierce advocates. Examples of vision statements for some of the most recognized brands, and even faith-based non-profits and churches, must have a vision so followers have a clear understanding of their role in the company, the community or God's kingdom:

IKEA

> *To create a better everyday life for the many people.*

Focus on the Family

> *Redeemed families, communities, and societies worldwide through Christ.*

Alzheimer's Association

> *A world without Alzheimer's.*

This quote from Andy Stanley, pastor and Christian author, says so much about the importance of Vision:

> *"When a plan or strategy fails, people are tempted to assume it was the wrong vision. Plans and strategies can always be changed and improved. But vision doesn't change. Visions are simply refined with time."*
> **Andy Stanley**

Now, onto the Mission Statement. The norm for the some of the most recognized brands is short and to-the-point:

Starbucks

> *To inspire and nurture the human spirit – one person, one cup and one neighborhood at a time.*

Google

> *Google's mission is to make the world's information more accessible for all users, including people with disabilities, such as visual impairment, color deficiency, and hearing impairment.*

Southwest

> *The mission of Southwest Airlines is dedication to the highest quality of Customer Service delivered with a sense of warmth, friendliness, individual pride, and Company Spirit.*

A chain of uniquely terrific grocery stores based in Monrovia, California, my old hometown, is Trader Joe's. If you've shopped in a Trader Joe's and conversed with any of the vibrant Hawaiian shirt-wearing employees about inventory, or during a cheese and cracker tasting at the back of the store, you wouldn't have to read the Mission to know exactly what the brand embodies:

Trader Joes

> *"The mission of Trader Joe's is to give our customers the best food and beverage values that they can find anywhere and to provide them with the information required to make informed buying decisions."*

Now that you see what some of the most recognized brands have written for their vision and mission, it's time to start thinking about your own brilliant statements and long term strategy. Here are some questions to ponder before you start the process with your team:

Vision: What do you want to be in future?
(This is, in effect, your dream.)

- Keywords for our company's vision statement:

Mission: What are you planning to accomplish to achieve your vision? (The details to achieve your dream.)

- Keywords for our company's mission statement:

Strategy: How do you plan to fulfill your mission?

- Keywords to include in our strategic plan, including emotions that you want employees and customers to feel.

Culture: What values and beliefs will you embrace? (This will help you with hiring, and also drive strategy and tactics.)

- What are our company values?

Your product or service offerings will be driven by your values and beliefs

- What core products and/or services do we currently offer?

- What should we offer?

Now, using your keywords and input from your committee, write out your company's vision and mission statements:

Our Company Vision

Our Company Mission

Soulful Strategy

Successful companies without a strategic plan make errors all the time. One expensive scenario is sending the marketing team out all alone in left field, charged with creating campaigns and executing advertising plans that are brilliant and within budget. The marketing director or VP falls in love with the campaign, sells it successfully to the owner of the company, and the team moves ahead and kicks-off the campaign.

> *Meanwhile, back in the real world… the sales force is not hitting goals, and the VP of sales and the CFO are wondering who approved the new campaign that does nothing to address driving traffic or leads, doesn't feature the higher margin staple products?*

The president and marketing team were all-in with the right side of their brains, moving full speed ahead and doing everything they think is best for the company. Just one little problem: they didn't bother to run it by any other department leaders.

Silos happen to good companies.

Marketing isn't the only party to blame here. The creative types usually get more than their fair share of finger pointing when things go wrong, and I know from experience that communication is a two-way street. If you're a vice president, director or manager of any department, get in the habit of in-person meetings and short phone calls to share information when things are going well, not just when the you-know-what has already hit the fan.

A strategic plan that is referred to weekly would have partly solved this problem. The VP or Director of Marketing should have gone to the other managers with details about the campaign idea long before taking the idea to the president for approval. Armed with knowledge of the current business climate and input from key stakeholders, the campaign would have been finessed based on fact-based reasons and then a solid, well-thought out campaign would have been presented to the president.

If you're not familiar with the term "silos" (which is very likely the case if you didn't grow up in a farming community, or you're one of a dozen people who aren't a fan of Chip, JoJo and their HGTV show "Fixer Upper"), you may be new to the world of business. The term "silo mentality" is defined in the Business Dictionary as *"A mind-set present in some companies when certain departments or sectors do not wish to share information with others in the same company."* The definition goes on to state that *"this type of mentality will reduce the efficiency of the overall operation, reduce morale, and may contribute to the demise of a productive company culture."*

As Stephanie Gravel, retired Deputy Director for Parks and Recreation in a large Los Angeles suburb, would eloquently say: "True dat."

Stephanie worked for over 20 years managing everything from the pools to the youth activities, community classes, and the annual 4th of July concert that drew over 10,000 people. In her role as Deputy Director she worked 50-60 hours a week, during the slow times. When it was concert season she'd go home only to sleep a few hours, shower, have a meal with her family and then head back to wear her talent manager and promoter hat. Along with dedicated supervisors and coordinators, and talented young people she trained and mentored each summer, the team tackled every project together.

Some of the stories she'd share about the bands hired to perform were so over-the-top I'd swear she was lying, or at least exaggerating, except for the fact that Stephanie was the poster child for honesty and integrity. A popular "one hit wonder" artist from the 1980s demanded over $1,000 worth of sushi for the band. After their set, they said they wanted it boxed up to go. (*Raw sushi? Boxed up after sitting around for five hours in the Los Angeles summer heat? Celebrities really do have different ways of living.*)

Silos were common where some officials were elected and roles were replaced every two or four years. The "regulars" who were hired and stayed for years and oftentimes decades knew how things were supposed to work in the city, but training all of the new municipal employees who might only be around for one term was still an important part of the job.

Any civic employee knows that silos are par for the course when working for the government. Stephanie was a master at breaking down silos, and when they couldn't be toppled, she'd figure out a work-around. Any company would be smart to hire her as a business consultant.

How to prevent silos? Easy. Start at the top. The CEO is the first person to blame for silos. If you're the CEO, this might hurt. But the truth sometimes does hurt. And yes, you can handle the truth. That's why you're in charge.

Rather than waste time on figuring out when things went south and interview all the team leaders individually to find out why they don't communicate with each other, do this: set up a meeting at the end of this week, or as soon as all of your department heads will be in the office. Start at 8:30 am with breakfast in your office or the conference room, and open the meeting with the announcement that you've let the team down, and that you're taking full responsibility for what you're about to say. Chances are they'll be shocked, and will wonder if you're quitting or closing down the business.

Next, tell them that there is a communication problem. And that it is stopping.

Right. Now.

No excuses. No blaming anyone. No looking back. Your rally speech might sound like this:

"Now is the time to break down the silos. Now is the time to starting being transparent. Now is the time to be open and honest with each other, and with our teams. We are not going to continue to put our heads in the sand and pretend there isn't a problem. Each one of you will meet with your teams after we finish up and present what we're discussing to your staff. We have a great company and good intentions, but we might be fooling ourselves about culture and about what our customers think about us."

Inform your leadership team that you'll set up a meeting within the next week to discuss the strategic plan, and encourage each officer, vice president and director to meet ahead of time and draft a list of concerns, ideas, hopes and goals to consider when working on the strategy. Let them know that the strategic plan will be a document that will help to break down silos, but is also being created so everyone is focused on the same goals, and that everyone at the company, at every level, is part of reaching the goals.

If you work for a company in a non-management role and recognize that silos are a problem, run - don't walk - to the CEO's office and ask for a meeting. Chances are the person in charge is aware of the situation, but in order to start breaking down the silos, why not share your concerns and offer to be part of the committee tasked with working on the strategic plan?

Strategic Planning Tips from a Successful Entrepreneur

Steve Robbins successfully grew his family's mall-based jewelry stores into a multi-market chain of specialty engagement ring stores. I had the privilege of working for Steve during some of the busiest growth phases for the company and consider my 12-plus years of experience at Robbins Brothers equivalent to earning an MBA. I'm blessed today to call Steve a mentor and friend.

Steve shared the following insights on strategy from his entrepreneurial perspective:

Good things happen when you know what you want and are willing to make a plan and execute it to achieve the result that you desire.

Strategy is that plan.

For entrepreneurs, "strategy" starts with three elements:

- *Me (the entrepreneur)*

- *The business itself*

- *The strategic plan*

1. ***The first element for "me" – the entrepreneur - is personal ownership.***

   WHAT DO I WANT AND WHAT ARE THE TRADE OFFS?

   What is it I want and am willing to contribute? What limitations do I have? Does this serve my overall life plan, and how might this affect those I love?

   What do I bring to the table? Think about resources like personal capabilities, passion, time, relationships, knowledge, capital or access to capital.

   How will I meet my obligations while cash flow doesn't allow me to take an income? Do I feel equipped to take on this challenge?

DOES MY BUSINESS IDEA HAVE A REASON TO BE?

The selection of what business I choose to be in is the critical factor on its potential success. I always try to ask myself THROUGH THE EYES OF MY CUSTOMER, "does this business idea have a reason to be?" Doing a perfect job of execution in the wrong business will not lead to a successful result. Doing a mediocre execution in the right business can be successful as you figure things out. If you have thoughtfully determined that, A) considering current and perceivable future competition that the business you want to be in has a reason for being; and B) that you are well equipped to pursue it and in doing so it fits into your life plan, then it will need a strategy that takes it where you want it to go.

2. *A COUPLE THINGS ABOUT STRATEGY:*

*Strategy is simply a plan that is intended to take you to your intended goals for the enterprise. It will break down the key steps to getting there. It will include determining what core competencies (or the key capabilities that will enable you or the enterprise to add special value) which you will need in order to achieve your plan. (Think of these as **key difference makers.**)*

*If these can be developed and integrated into a strategy that gives you an advantage over competitors in serving your clients and this advantage and or new ones you develop can be sustained over time, **then your business likely has a chance to be successful.***

Note that developing the strategy requires breaking down each key element and identifying the resources needed in a time dated plan.

How to Write the Strategic Plan for Your Organization

An effective strategy for a family-owned business or start-up entrepreneurial company should fit onto 10 pages or less, and though the planning stages shouldn't be rushed, the final document will be simple and make sense to even the newest employee – or a prospective investor. It should include:

- Your vision
- Your mission statement
- A company description (two or three sentences)
- Your organization's values, i.e. what you stand for, in a few bullet points
- Competitive landscape
- Chart with your strengths, weaknesses, opportunities and threats (SWOT)
- Financial Projections, sales goals and plans (3 bullet points, max) for each division
- Marketing plan
- Service or Merchandise/Product plans
- Operations/Facilities Plan
- IT Plan
- Web/ecommerce plan
- Other division plans that pertain to your business
- Personnel: Annual budget and Organizational chart

Who to include on the strategic planning committee:

Include the executives, but also invite at least two non-execs (I recommend one non-exec for every 25-50 employees at your company) who are natural leaders, have proven mentoring skills, and have the respect of their peers. This committee should include people who represent the brand well and who have been with the company long enough to understand all of the good, bad and ugly. Optimistic committee members are important, but they shouldn't have their head in the clouds and be ignorant as to what is going on within the company, the industry and the community.

Where do I start?

Templates for strategic plans can found online, and most can be downloaded for free. Several business experts state in different ways that you wouldn't set out on a long road trip without a map or navigation, and that a smart business leader wouldn't run a business without a map showing the team how to reach their goals over the next 1-5 years.

SOULFUL TIP:

Think of your strategy as a road map that will take your company on the most profitable path to your destination

Forbes.com has an excellent and in-depth overview on how to write your own strategic plan, written by contributor and self-proclaiming serial entrepreneur Dave Lavinsky. The 13 sections would apply to an organization that has some experience with planning, but it is a worthwhile read for any executive or person who wants to be in management. Dave is the co-founder and president of Growthink and has helped over 100,000 businesses with their growth plans. The full article can be found at www.forbes.com/sites/davelavinsky, along with the template that is available for purchase.

In addition to the items listed earlier in this chapter, Growthink suggests including the following in your strategic plan:

- Executive Summary
- Elevator Pitch
- Key Performance Indicators ("KPIs")
- Target Customers
- Industry Analysis

Gazelles.com offers a one-page strategic plan (OPSP) form that is editable and that will provide a solid place to start for a small company, or one that is just starting out.

<u>https://gazelles.com/g/one-page-tools/strategy</u>

Simply fill in the "Reputation Drivers" (also known as People), which will always include employees and customers, but may also be comprised of shareholders, vendors, or sponsors. You'll then populate the form with your core values/beliefs, your purpose (the "Why" you do what you do), your long-term target dates for where you want to be in 3-5 years, your short-term goals for the next year, and goes on to ask for Actions, KPIs and Key Initiatives.

If you're the leader at a non-profit organization, the strategic plan will differ in some areas as you'll be seeking out resources and donors versus generating revenue from products sold or services provided. NOLO is an excellent source for tips and information and has a section on their website dedicated to nonprofit organizations.

Go to <u>http://www.nolo.com/</u> and enter "create a strategic plan for your nonprofit" in the search bar.

Your strategy needn't be complicated. If this is your organization's first go at writing a strategic plan, keep it simple and focus on just the next 12 – 24 months. Go back to it every couple of weeks and revise if necessary during the first year. When you have a clear picture of your goals and you've assigned a point person to own the strategic plan for your company, you can then finesse the details and review quarterly with the team.

Just remember to include the emotional details that make your brand or service stand out from the competition. In a word, keep the strategy "soulful."

I'll close this chapter on strategy with a quote from the late, great business genius Steve Jobs who was chairman, CEO and co-founder of Apple. (Note that the word "strategy" isn't even mentioned below.)

> *"People think focus means saying yes to the thing you've got to focus on. But that's not what it means at all. It means saying no to the hundred other good ideas that there are. You have to pick carefully."*

> Steve Jobs

REBOOT

The very first video played on MTV was "Video Killed the Radio Star." You've undoubtedly read about the death of the retail brick-and-mortar store and wonder what other industries Amazon will buy-out and make part of their Prime offering.

But keep in mind that the retail store is not dead. Amazon has been opening book and tech stores in major markets. Furniture stores such as At Home, Ashley and America's Furniture Warehouse are expanding into new markets, responding to customers who desire to see, touch and try-out sofas, dining sets and mattresses.

America's Best Contacts and Eyeglasses has seen growth for several years and, after opening stores in the impossibly tough business state of California, priced their initial public offering (IPO) at $18-$22 (October 2017) and then saw the stock price quickly rise to over $30. Reade Fahs, CEO of National Vision, America's Best parent company, made the financial show rounds and explained how his stores would compete with online eyeglass darling Warby Parker. Mr. Reade confidently stated that the eyes need to be checked by a licensed eyecare professional and that they aren't just selling tools to correct vision. They are providing a medical service that can with early detection of tumors, cataracts and other health challenges that an online store will never catch.

America's Best stores offer low priced eyeglasses and contacts and are conveniently located in strip malls and near big box stores. Walk-in business is welcome along with patients who make appointments. Instead of panicking and changing their business model to compete with online players, America's Best put a stake in the ground and decided that being the store with an eye doctor on staff is what made them different.

Reboot

This third step to offering the Soulful Experience will require that you look at your organization in new ways. Working on the following four tasks you'll be, in effect, rebooting your company.

1. First, you'll go over the **research.** This is the information you gathered in Steps 1 and 2 and will include research on the industry, the community, customer needs and your current employee structure.
2. Then, you'll **reorganize.** You'll look at leadership first, then the entire organizational chart. You may find everyone is doing what they were born to do, or you might decide to change things around.
3. After that, you'll **revise.** See if there are too many products or not enough. Or, not enough of the right products. Is the service you're providing relevant in today's world and in your local community? How is the store or showroom design? Is there a consistent user experience across all platforms, from digital (phone, tablet, laptop) to bricks and mortar, sponsorships, partnerships and events? Does the tone, voice and style of your advertising match what customers will experience online and in your stores?
4. And finally, when you finish with the research, reorganize the team and revise what you provide, it will be time to **revitalize.** Not only the customer experience, but the employee morale. Find a positive, genuine culture that fits your organization like a glove and is understood internally and externally.

RESEARCH

Review your notes on the competition from Steps One and Two. What are competitors doing in your community? Secret shop them, take notes, and visit their website. If the space is crowded with other competitors, such as beauty salons or restaurants, go to Google, type in your product or service, and visit the locations that have the best - and most - reviews.

Be sure to look outside of your industry for best-in-class stores, too. Consumers have limited time and financial resources, and you need to know where they are spending their money and why.

Review your customers' comments online and in-house surveys.

If human resources hasn't provided the employee sentiment yet, have them write up a summary. Be sure to include feedback gathered from exit interviews as well as Glassdoor.com and even in a Google search of your company name. (Employees may tweet frustrations or share pics on Instagram of a bad day at the office or store.)

The research phase is also the time you'll gather customer testimonials, traditions about the owners who started the business, facts about your product and services, and hopefully uncover some folklore. The end result? Stories about your brand that you'll share in advertising, on your website and social media, in job postings and with vendors.

BRAND STORY: REI

REI – What happens when a specialty outdoor retailer closes its doors on one of the biggest shopping days of the year? The employees get Black Friday off to enjoy biking, skiing, surfing, hiking or whatever outdoor sport they love, and customers are encouraged to do the same.

This wasn't just a genius marketing idea. It was authentic to the brand. And it didn't come cheap. REI paid all 12,000 employees NOT to work the day after Thanksgiving. It took a huge risk by telling customers that instead of spending money at REI on Black

Friday, to #OptOutside and spend time with friends or family in the great outdoors.

This brand story is so anti-retail that it is shocking REI took such a leap of faith chance in 2015. But over 1.4 million people took the suggestion to go outside instead of shop at crowded malls and shared the Opt Outside hashtag (#OptOutside) on social media. An estimated 100+ retailers also closed for business on Black Friday, following REI's lead. And to anyone who disses public relations as a waste of time, note that this campaign had 2.7 BILLION PR impressions. That is some valuable media, especially during Q4, the most expensive time of year to buy TV, radio, print and digital advertising.

The company continues to benefit from this "what if" idea, proposed by a merchandise director in a meeting. Millennials, Gen X-ers and Baby Boomers who are outdoor enthusiasts tend to look at traditional advertising as bogus. Anyone who runs 10Ks, hikes 14ers or snowboards double-black diamond runs is likely to be suspicious of a chain that hires models to wear jackets that are made for trekking across Antarctica.

REI's mission, and the culture that has been created over the years, provided a foundation that made this phenomenal brand story possible:

"At REI, we inspire, educate and outfit for a lifetime of outdoor adventure and stewardship"

The fact that this concept came not from the marketing team, but from the merchandise director, reminds us that when everyone in the organization knows what the brand stands for and the vision and mission are clear, great things are bound to happen.

REORGANIZE

Making objective changes to the employee structure is challenging at the best of companies, but it is perhaps toughest to do at a small, family managed organization. Your spouse or brother-in-law may have been running the financials since you started, but if the business has evolved from one store to three, or if revenue has quadrupled, your business can't thrive without a professional controller.

Review your vision, mission and strategic plan from the prior chapter again. Now, create your "dream" organizational chart with titles only, not specific names of employees.

Next, look at job descriptions for each title (if you have an HR manager or team, have them provide the descriptions along with typical education and salary for the position) and schedule a meeting to review.

Write next to each title the name of the employee who currently holds the position, and then with a red pen, write down the name of who you think should be in that position, if someone different. If it is a new position, write "TBD" and highlight it.

Are you surprised by anything? Do any titles remain blank that need to be filled from the outside? Are there any employees left without titles? The goal here isn't to eliminate any dedicated team members, but instead to match up the qualified person with the title that will take your company in the right direction. A longtime, loyal employee who doesn't fit into the new organization chart can be trained and educated, and will be grateful for the opportunity to grow in a new field.

SOULFUL TIP

Establish a mentoring program that is geared to help employees work toward a position that fulfills their "calling." Pair up executives with employees in a year-long partnership.

REVISE

If your company is threatened by online players, devise a strategy to change the game. Give customers a reason to come to your store.

- *Is your store or showroom design relevant to today's shoppers? This doesn't mean trendy nor does it have to be super expensive to make updates. Your brand needs to be consistent across all platforms and you can make design changes in phases if your budget is limited. Can't hire an architect and contractor this year? That is fine, but do consider investing in an architectural design firm (WD Partners in Columbus is experienced with showrooms, retail, restaurants and grocery) to establish budget and timelines, then gradually make the changes over months or even a couple of years. Your digital assets can be updated alongside with your physical buildings, products and ancillary materials for trade shows, partnerships and events.*
- *Consider subleasing a corner of your retail store to a local coffee roaster and sell specialty drinks. On select days or during "happy hour" on a traditionally slow day, you could offer free drinks. Happy hour can be 9-10 am, too.*
- *If you sell clothing, bring in a seamstress and put this craftsperson front and center. Offer free alterations for items purchased at your store and charge for outside items.*
- *Host a signature event every week or month, whatever frequency makes sense and whatever you can afford without cutting into profits. Create a place where customers and their friends can gather.*
- *Take a cue from Nordstrom and Brighton and turn your salespeople into personal shoppers. Hire employees who have incredible personalities first, then train them to make connections with customers, to develop relationships, and to make customers feel like celebrities by having outfits ready to try on, special pieces set aside and held for a few days until the customer can come in, and host VIP parties for customers at your store.*
- *Partner with another business that complements what you do and cross-promote each other.*
  - o *Luxury car dealer: connect with the top jeweler in your area and host try-on parties at your dealership, and*

park your newest model cars in front of the jewelry store during key holidays and designer events

o   *Real Estate Agent: stage your homes with furniture from the local home furnishings store*

o   *Shoe Store: create window displays showing the current styles with entire outfits from a local clothing boutique, and have the boutique display your shoes in their windows for the ultimate cross-promotion*

Restaurants:

- *Farm-to-Table can be offered at even fast-food places. Start visiting farmer's markets or go straight to local ranches and farms to source different options on your menu.*
- *Lease a food truck and take your restaurant to concerts, workplaces and special events.*
- *Host a smaller version of your restaurant with a "pop-up" restaurant with your chef in people's homes, with invitations to the social media elite.*
- *What type of customers do you want? Host "new menu" events and invite your followers and influencers in the community who fit your target profile*
- *Invite the local food critics to come in and experience your restaurant, meet the chef, etc.*

REVITALIZE

This is where you'll really have fun, as long as you have the rule that there are no rules.

Revitalize means to refresh, revive, rejuvenate. Even the best companies do this, but a company that needs to improve its experience will reap the most benefits when deciding to change things up in a major way.

What is required to improve employee morale?

Some think it is free breakfast every Friday, or a 401k match, or getting your birthday off as a paid holiday. But morale isn't based on getting things. It is a matter of respect and treating the employees the way you want to be treated.

If your receptionist needs to take an afternoon off to take her child to the doctor, she shouldn't have to be docked four hours of pay, nor should she have to take sick time. If you or another executive take time off, paid, to attend to a family matter, be sure you extend the same courtesy to every team member.

Employee morale is also dependent on kindness, respect, and transparency. Greet everyone you see, learn people's first names, find out what they do outside of work. Do what Dan Calkins, President and COO at Benjamin Moore does, and join your team during the lunch hour in the cafeteria or kitchen. Sit down with the folks who work in the factory or in quality control and get to know them. If the television is on and the group has a regular show they watch, watch it with them, ask questions and become a fan.

Hold regular meetings and invite everyone to join you for weekly or monthly updates. Be transparent whenever possible, and you'll not only raise morale, you'll create a team that is passionate about working for your company.

As for your customers, make it mandatory that every executive interacts with customers on a regular basis. Visit your stores, eat at the restaurants, ride the rides with those very important people who pay to do business with you. Stay in touch with the front lines and support those who directly support the customers every way you can.

AND BACK TO TRANSPARENCY...

Once you have your vision, mission and strategy in place, host informal meetings where you invite small groups of employees to meet the CEO or another executive in their office for coffee and dessert. Share what you've been doing, the reason for shaking things up, and let the teams know that formal announcements and training will be part of the next phase. This level of transparency, coming from a member of the leadership team, will help to build trust and break down silos. Simple communication on a regular basis is what best-in-class companies do, and is an easy, no-cost way to help create a positive, genuine culture.

SOULFUL LEADERSHIP

The first chapter in Deuteronomy describes the appointing of leaders (verses 12 - 15) to take the burden off of a single person. Designating leaders who would oversee groups of different sizes made Moses a more effective leader, and delegating responsibilities based on each leaders' strengths made the people even stronger as a whole.

Leadership is a trait many feel they are born with, or with the right education have earned the right to the title after their name. But it is the wise CEO who follows the lead of Moses and appoints leaders based on their strengths. If you run a family business, or consider members of your management team close friends, this is the time you need to review the current organizational chart again. Yes, you did this in the last chapter, but this will give you an opportunity to focus specifically on leadership at your company.

Find a quiet place, close the door, and start with a few blank sheets of paper. Warning: this assignment might seem unbearable, especially if you're one who prefers to avoid conflict. But it is crucial if you want to move your brand from average to Soulful.

If you run a medium or large organization and aren't familiar with all the leaders at your company, do this exercise with the names of your direct reports. Ask your VPs to then do the exercise with the names of managers who report to them.

1. Write down the names of every officer, vice president and director, and then answer the following questions:
    -   What are three positive traits about each person?
    -   How does each trait make him/her qualified for the position he/she holds?

- List at least one major contribution each senior leader has made that positively impacted the growth of the business in the past six months.
- How has each team member contributed to the financial success of the company in the past year?

2. Write down the name of the person you consider the second-in-command, regardless of current title:

3. List the names of three employees (managers or non-managers) who contributed to the growth of the company over the past two years:

4. Think about three employees (managers or non-managers) who have led major changes in your organization in recent years (i.e budgetary, IT, POS, product offering, advertising re-vamp, customer service, etc.) and add their names here.

5. Name three people in your organization who are running multiple projects or teams.

6. Who are three employees (managers or non-managers) who you would trust to run the company if you suddenly had to take off for six months?

Look at the names on your sheets and see if there is any overlap. Does anything surprise you?

Now, write down the titles of your direct reports, without any specific names. (CFO, VP of Marketing, etc.) Be sure to include titles for positions that you'd like to fill in the next 12 months, too.

Next to each title, write a few words or bullet points to describe this position.

- What name or names come to mind for each title, based on your description?

- Is there a name of someone who doesn't work for you (perhaps a contact at another company, or a speaker at a conference who was a subject-matter expert) that fits the description?

- Did you come up blank with an individual's name for any titles?

If the names of your current executives came up when you wrote out the descriptions, then it appears you have the right management team running your organization. However, odds are that at least one title didn't match up with the person in that current role. This is common for small organizations and family businesses, for the following reasons:

- You (or the CEO) wants/likes/demands total control.

- Family members have been in management positions since the company started

- The managers have been loyal through thick and thin and they've earned the title

- It's going to be impossible to find people who are trustworthy and we don't want to fix what isn't broken

53

The tough question: Do you have the right people in leadership positions? A fairly common approach to a family business is for a patriarch or matriarch to appoint siblings or adult children to take on operations, sales, product development, finance, purchasing, marketing, merchandising and even working the phones and cash register in the early growth stages. The logic is that these family members may own part of the company now or in the future, and therefore can do multiple jobs and don't expect the same salary that someone hired from off the street would demand.

A member of the family working as an employee or business partner has another added benefit: trust that has been built over time.

But ask yourself this? How many companies have failed because family members or trusted managers weren't qualified for the roles they held? According to JSA Advising, *"only **30 percent** of all family-owned businesses survive into the second generation and only **12 percent** will survive into the third generation. Surprisingly, only **3 percent** of all family businesses operate at the fourth generation and beyond."*

Small businesses, family-owned or not, have unique challenges. When your staff is small, you likely don't have an HR specialist with corporate experience helping you manage job performance and employee reviews. Human resources, hiring, and firing oftentimes falls on the shoulders of the CEO at a company with less than 50 employees.

Pride is one culprit that prevents most of us from admitting we're not doing something right. Since our identity tends to be tied up in our career, it is unrealistic - though not totally unheard of - to expect a person to come forward and state that they're not the right person for a job. When this person is related to the owner or CEO, there might be a not-so-transparent veil that covers up the fact that the family member or friend is actually hurting the company.

If you suspect that you don't have the right leaders in place, meet with your human resources manager to start a process on personnel reorganization. If you don't have an HR manager, ask other CEOs in your circle if they can recommend a consultant to come in and help. Though the thought of letting employees go may cause stress, the goal here is not to fire anyone, but instead to move trusted managers to positions that are better suited to their skills and leadership strengths.

In rare cases, you might learn that an executive who isn't qualified for the position is also not trustworthy, or has a management style that hasn't been in line with the culture and therefore has high turnover on his team. This would be a valuable lesson to learn sooner than later. Better to let this person go and find a replacement who fits in with your culture, has the experience and education for the position, and has outstanding leadership qualities.

The Three "Cs" of Executive Leadership

Regardless of whether or not you have the ideal executive team in place at this very moment, have laser-focused (they don't have to be long and dragged out) meetings twice a week, in your office, with a specific agenda that addresses your company's current challenges and goals. The sooner you get everyone on board with your vision, the sooner you can start developing your executives with what I call the three Cs of leadership: **credibility, consistency** and **clarity**.

CREDIBILITY (the quality of being trusted and believed in) is an absolute for any person leading a team. The executive leaders must be above reproach, which means that when they accept a senior role at your company, they must always behave in a manner that demonstrates trust, honors your values, and cannot be interpreted by anyone within or outside the organization as inappropriate. This individual represents your brand, and is expected to be a brand ambassador for everyone you employ, your vendors, your customers, and the community.

The late Dr. Billy Graham, one of the most recognized and respected evangelists in the world, stated once that when he traveled for his ministry, he would not enter an elevator with his secretary unless another person was also present. This eliminated any chance of rumors or perceived wrongdoing and protected the reputations of both the pastor and his female employee.

This is an excellent lesson for any employee, and also can prevent lawsuits and negative publicity.

(Please do not take this as a directive to only hire "perfect" people. You'll never find anyone to fill in your top positions, and you'll overlook top candidates who may have made mistakes in the past, but are now on the right track to demonstrating credibility.)

Take the initiative and draft a document that clearly outlines what Credibility means at your company. Review it with the HR team - and a lawyer - to make sure you're aren't discriminating against any potential or current employees and that the guidelines adhere to state and federal laws. Your document might look like this:

Management Credibility Guidelines

As an executive or manager at XYZ company, you'll be expected to conduct yourself in a professional manner at all times when at the office, branches/stores/restaurants, warehouses, company events, with vendors and at dinners and community events where you're representing the company.

- No swearing, yelling, gossiping or demeaning of anyone
- No excessive alcohol consumption (one drink per hour, max. If you start to feel tipsy, switch to non-alcoholic beverage.)
- Married employees are not permitted to have any romantic relationships with employees, vendors or customers
- Single employees who are supervisors or managers may not date anyone who reports to them or reports to another manager.
- Illegal drug use, or abuse of prescription drugs, is not acceptable at any time.

Work with your HR team, executive leadership or a trusted consultant to discuss how to take action if a manager doesn't comply with one or more of the items on the list. Rather than termination, I believe that it is best to set up a program to coach the individual and give him/her opportunities to correct the problem.

In the example of a manager dating an employee, I knew of a couple who met at the workplace and when they realized there was chemistry and they wanted to start dating, one of them found a job at a different company so they could date and not jeopardize their jobs. Last I heard they were happily married for several years and had two kids.

Romance is inevitable when you have a significantly sized staff, but it is important to make sure that you are set up to protect your employees as well as the company.

CONSISTENCY (conformity in the application of something, typically that which is necessary for the sake of logic, accuracy, or fairness)

True story: I had a boss who scheduled weekly meetings with his direct reports, yet at least half of the meetings he arrived late or forgot about the meeting altogether. That was bad, but not as bad as blaming his assistant for not rescheduling, or coming in late, complaining that he works until 7:30 every night and blaming everyone else for keeping him late. Most meetings had no agenda, and often times we couldn't get through the small group's updates in an hour. The meetings were unorganized and unproductive, and rather than review action items discussed in a prior meeting, we had to repeat what we had already covered the week before. Early on at this company I realized something was amiss, and soon learned there was not a strategic plan to be found anywhere in the building. And this was a company with over 800 employees.

Wanting to help, and understanding that several of the top executives were overwhelmed, I offered to draft a strategic plan for our department, which would at least be a starting point to get the company as whole on the right track in the future. What I found out however was that they had a Powerpoint sheet with three tactics, and the C-Suite truly believed that this was the strategy for the company.

Meetings and strategic plans are important, yes. If these were the only two areas that lacked consistency, they wouldn't be so different from most other companies, right? But three executives in the C-Suite were inconsistent in just about every area of the business, from the way they managed the budget, to sharing information with the teams, to personnel issues. Others looked to the people with the important titles to right wrongs and fulfill promises, but it didn't take long to realize that the only thing that was consistent about the company was how inconsistently the place was managed.

Despite making millions of dollars each month and having a couple of departments run efficiently due to experienced individuals at the helm, the key team leaders didn't provide consistent leadership. Over 25% of the team's personnel - including directors, managers and some incredibly talented and very experienced employees - quit within a span of two months.

Lack of consistency was the primary reason for the mass exodus.

CLARITY (the quality of being clear; coherence and intelligibility).

My dad and I had the same conversation all the time when I was 15 and started driving with my permit. He'd be in the passenger seat and as soon as I turned the ignition on and asked if he wanted me to go straight to the destination, he'd jokingly reply, "You can't go straight there. You need to turn left at the stop sign, then right at the light, then go up the road for two miles, then you turn right in the parking lot."

Being literal can be annoying, especially to a teenager. But my dad made a valid point and wanted me to understand that specific stops and turns would be required before we could reach the grocery store, mall or bank. It isn't so different when you're leading a company.

A leader who refers to the strategy on a daily basis will be known for clarity and the team will understand the manager's directions when there is a strategic plan in writing. Will scenarios come up that weren't planned? Absolutely, you can bet on it. And in these circumstances, a leader must still direct the team and be precise with the end goals. The way your team gets to the finish line doesn't necessarily matter, as long as they follow company policy and don't cut corners or do anything to compromise the project or the brand.

Best-selling author John C. Maxwell has said there are five myths about leadership. The first one, The Management Myth, is explained as follows:

> *"A widespread misunderstanding is that leading and managing is one and the same.*
>
> *Up until a few years ago, books that claimed to be about leadership were often about management. The main difference between the two is that leadership is about influencing people to follow, while management focuses on maintaining systems and processes. The best way to test whether a person can lead rather than just manage is to ask him to create positive change. Managers can maintain direction, but they can't change it. To move people in a new direction, you need influence."*
>
> *John C. Maxwell*
> *Leadership 101 – What Every Leader Needs to Know*

Today many brands work with professional "influencers" (sometimes known as bloggers or social media stars) in advertising campaigns and storytelling on the website. The fashion world is one that is using influencers effectively. Popular magazines *Vogue* and *InStyle* feature influencers with street style in fashion layouts, on pages next to famous highly paid supermodels and actresses. Influencers who have a few thousand or a few million followers are invited to red carpet events, galas and grand openings, and sit in the front row next to Anna Wintour at the runway shows in Paris, New York and Milan. These influencers aren't managing the clothing lines or magazines, but they are attracting followers to the brands and making six-figure incomes in the process. Are they leaders in the office? No. But they are directing and inspiring fans to shop for the products they endorse, wear or clap for, and as a result they are indeed leaders.

Your leadership team can learn from these influencers, and although you may not be a peer in terms of age or socioeconomic background, you absolutely need to find a common ground. The sooner you can find out what makes you an important character in your brand's story, the sooner you'll become an influencer to employees and customers.

TIPS TO BECOME A SOULFUL LEADER

Think back to a boss, teacher or another person in your life who mentored you not because he or she would get anything out of it, but because it was the right thing to do for you. This mentor had what you might call the heart of a servant. My former boss who I mentioned earlier in this book, Steve Robbins, has been and continues to be my mentor.

I met with Steve and his lovely wife Marisa for breakfast on their patio on a recent warm summer morning and enjoyed coffee, donuts and pastries, as we reminisced about how hard we worked for the several years he owned the business, and also how much we grew together. Good times, and some very hard times. Long hours and many weekends, a requisite for any entrepreneurial organization in growth mode.

But we were always learning and more importantly, making a difference in our customers' lives *and* also in each other's lives.

If the Urban Dictionary ever needs a photo to place next to the term "work family" they may just use a picture that shows our entire team back in the heyday, confident in knowing that we accomplished more together as a united front than any single one of us could have done on our own.

Teamwork was not just a buzzword tossed around at meetings. We lived and breathed teamwork on a daily basis, we had each other's backs all the time, and the company thrived as a result.

As much as my very humble former boss didn't want to accept our thanks and praises for his outstanding leadership, there was no denying that he built an organization that encouraged each person to live up to his or her full potential. There are **six key things** he did as a **Soulful Leader** that positively impacted the company and made us successful as an organization, as well as fostered our individual professional success:

A Soulful Leader:

1. **Allows employees to make mistakes.** Many workplaces have an atmosphere of fear, which is a surefire way to suck any creativity out of the organization. Steve had a saying: "If you're not making mistakes, you're not growing. And if you're not growing, you're not helping the business grow." That's not to say we could repeat our mistakes more than once or twice, but as long as we learned from it and corrected the error, we'd be forgiven and didn't have to fear that we'd lose our job.

2. **Acknowledges the team's effort when and where it matters:** Give credit to the person or team where credit is due, and share the praises with the board of directors, the management team, peers and vendors.

3. **Personally thanks employees** for a job well done, in person, on the phone or with a handwritten card.

4. **Is passionate and persistent about strategy**, and makes sure every employee understands the company's short and long-term goals. A Soulful Leader isn't afraid to be transparent, either, and will share the truth about financials, competitive challenges or problems in the organization when appropriate.

5. **Teaches others how to be effective communicators**. To listen and be present when in meetings, on the phone and even in hallway catch-ups.

6. **Creates a culture of "giving back" to the company and the community**, and practices what he or she preaches by doing the right thing, being generous, and setting positive examples _even when people aren't looking_.

Soulful Leaders are rare. If you're lucky enough to work for a leader who possesses the above character traits, stay put and count your blessings. If you don't have a Soulful Leader at your company, go to HR and ask if there are any leadership training programs planned for the management team. If you have a good relationship with one of the executives, go straight to the top, share the list of six key things to be a Soulful Leader with the CEO, the COO or another member in the C-suite and ask if you can do anything to help take leadership – and your company culture – in a new, positive direction.

And remember, no matter your title or position in the company, YOU can be a Soulful example to others. Leaders aren't defined by a corner office, or a parking space. Be the leader who inspires others, starting today, and spread some much-needed joy in your workplace.

THE IMPORTANCE OF MENTORING

I touched on mentoring earlier in this chapter, but it is imperative that you understand the "why" behind having a servant's heart in the workplace. A mentor is described as "an experienced or trusted adviser" who trains and counsels others. This person is more valuable than any diploma, certificate or college degree. If you haven't shown your appreciation to the mentor in your life up to this point, stop reading this and call or write a thank you note right now.

Mentors aren't just older, wiser experts in a field. They are intrinsically wired to come alongside others and be a guide. Mentors are oftentimes the smartest employees in the company, yet so humble that they don't always get recognized by upper management with titles or big offices. If you're lucky you'll have a chance in your career to work for a CEO who is a also a mentor.

Management training at a Soulful Company must include a program that prepares mentors at all levels. A company that invests in a formal mentoring program will have a pool of elite employees at all times. Retention rates will go up. Employee morale will improve. This is not a promise. This is a fact.

Investopedia listed some of the most successful corporate mentoring programs at Fortune 500 companies. General Electric places new college graduates into their Experienced Commercial Leadership Program, while Intel pairs up employees based on their skills and encourages team growth within the company. Employees get valuable training as well as gain insight on how to move up the ladder. According to Entrepreneur.com, *"a 2013 Vestrics study examined responses from more than 830 mentees and 670 mentors who participated in Sun Microsystem's program. Employee retention rates climbed 69 percent for the mentors and 72 percent for the mentees over the seven-year period of the study. The increased retention resulted in a savings of $6.7 billion in avoided staff turnover and replacement costs."*

The Journal of Vocational Behavior, in a 2013 study, found that mentors experience greater job satisfaction and a higher commitment to the employer. A mentoring program is a win/win/win for the employer, the employee mentor and the employee mentee.

Identify employees who are already mentoring others and invite them to be part of the committee that sets up your mentor program. It won't take long to find these individuals. Just look for the people who have other employees come to the desk or office daily with questions and who offer encouraging words to other associates in meetings. *Inc. com* lists the following key qualities of an effective mentor:

- Ability and willingness to communicate what you know
- Preparedness
- Approachability, availability, and the ability to listen
- Honesty with diplomacy

- Inquisitiveness
- Objectivity and fairness
- Compassion and genuineness

While a good manager should be a mentor (but truth be told, very few managers make the time to mentor), be sure to also look outside the management team for your mentors. Not every person who is a natural at mentoring will want to get into management, but these individuals should be recognized for their skills that are above and beyond the daily work that is outlined in their job description.

When you implement a formal mentoring program at your company, you'll create positive change by:

- Giving some of your best non-management employees who are mentors a reason to stay at your organization long-term
- Giving prospective hires a reason to apply and accept a position at your organization
- Improving productivity
- Improving employee morale and the overall company culture
- Increasing employee retention rates, thereby saving money in recruiting, training and turnover.

CREATE A CULTURE WHERE IT IS OKAY TO AGREE TO DISAGREE

Any strong company that is focused on growth will have managers and employees who disagree on things as mundane as what snacks to stock in the lunch room to big issues such as the budget and monthly sales goals. This is healthy and should reassure the CEO that you don't have only "yes" men and women working for you. (Be wary of a culture that is all about saying "yes" to everything recommended by the C-Suite. If you suspect this sounds like your organization, start asking the tough questions of your most trusted employees and peers.)

I recently watched a documentary by Benjamin Wagner titled

"Mister Rogers & Me" from 2012. I recommend it to anyone who needs a reminder on basic manners, acknowledging others' feelings, and allowing people around you to feel comfortable for just being themselves.

Tim Russert, the firm yet kind journalist who interviewed the world's most prominent people on his show "Meet the Press" for 16 years until his sudden passing in 2008, was a longtime friend of Mister Rogers. When interviewed for the documentary, he was asked what resonated about his time spent with the famous children's public television show host. Russert stated that we need to learn how to agree to disagree.

So simple. Something we learn as youngsters, yet somehow we forget as we grow up and become adults. Yet imagine what your office might be like if everyone was taught how to "agree to disagree." Wouldn't this be worth the time and expense to have a four-hour coaching session, with a trainer well-versed on this subject, and groups that break out into small groups for role playing?

Mister Rogers also told the young documentarian, who was a successful producer at MTV in its heyday, that the best thing you can offer to anyone is to just be yourself. Words of wisdom that are timeless. And apply not only to a school classroom filled with children, but also to a conference room with smart, successful and college-educated adults sitting around the table.

Remember the book *"All I Really Need to Know I Learned in Kindergarten"* by Robert Fulghum? This is on my list of "must read books" for executives. Just like Mr. Rogers taught us as kids, Robert Fulghum reminds us as adults. The principles and life lessons that were important in our childhood should be just as important in the business world. And remember, everyone who works for you is watching what you do as a leader.

> *"It doesn't matter what you say you believe –*
> *it only matters what you do."*
> Robert Fulghum

READY. SET. GO!

Now that you have your vision, mission and strategy in place and you're confident that your leadership roles are filled by individuals qualified and with aptitude and passion for the positions, it is time to take the first steps to getting The Soulful Experience into action.

Appoint each leader to head up a committee that oversees the following:

- Drafting and finalizing a 12-month calendar with bullet points and key action items (based on strategic plan) for each department
- Developing the game plan to roll out strategy to all team members
- Coaching team leaders to assign KPIs to every employee, with specific tasks and deadlines

MARKETING

- Designate a wall or a conference room as "the strategy area" and put every piece of collateral up that is customer and employee-facing. Look at each item through the lens of your new experience.

All Customer and Vendor-Facing Materials

- In-store (signage, brochures, forms, POS)
- Website

- Digital
- E-commerce
- Emails
- Mail (direct mail, catalogs, credit, letterhead, thank you cards, all other correspondence)
- Finance (letters to vendors, invoices, etc.)
- Boilerplate (for press releases and website)

All Employee/HR documents

- New hire packets
- Insurance
- Benefits (retirement, etc.)
- Company online portals
- Paychecks
- All correspondence (internal and external)

Every department will need to go through **all** paperwork, digital screens, contents in boxes and packets to ensure that any "old" messaging about your brand is replaced with copy that supports your focus on the experience.

THE STRATEGIC CALENDAR

There is a famous quote about a certain place of evil being paved with good intentions. Being a positive person who prefers solutions, I coined this quote:

"Good intentions without an action plan will leave you in the desert. Good intentions combined with a timeline and accountability partners will take you to the mountaintop."

Recently I had a small deck built in the backyard. The plans were simple, the materials were readily available, and the contractor and I agreed on the price and completion date. Four months later, after the agreed upon date, I'm texting and calling, practically begging the contractor to just finish already! Not that this is acceptable behavior by any means, but I've paid for the materials and for 50% of the work. The deck is now about 70% completed, but I'm left with a partial bench and no railings, so it is unusable for the most part.

Imagine going to your doctor and scheduling surgery. You work out the insurance details, get the x-rays and the pre-op tests out of the way. The day of surgery comes and you arrive at the hospital, change into your gown and soon you're getting the IV feed and speaking with the anesthesiologist and nurses who explain the procedure. Before you know it, you're coming out of the fog and you ask how the operation went, only to find out the doctor didn't finish the surgery! Your doctor had good intentions. He thought he came prepared. But as it turns out, one little piece of surgical equipment was missing and even though they cut you open, the cyst that was to be removed is still inside you. What should have been completed is in fact not finished, and you have to go through yet another procedure.

Of course, this is farfetched and highly unlikely. But why is it acceptable to drag out a project in the construction world or in the corporate world? It shouldn't be, right? A project that starts without a firm timeline, finish date, budget and plan of action is a project that isn't actually ready to start.

It is crucial that everyone at your organization understands the importance of a strategic calendar, and a calendar that is specific to each department which rolls up into the overall strategy. Assign project leaders and accountability partners to keep projects on schedule. If a deadline is in jeopardy, alert the team right away and have a brainstorm session to decide who can be brought on board to get the project back on track. You can create a simple calendar with a timeline in Excel for the key departments, and distribute to each team member.

Internal: Training

Do you have any positive memories of training? Jot down those places that provided you with a list of expectations, a well-defined job description, and graciously allowed you the time to settle in at the company. Did human resources or your manager give you a handbook and show you a video about the company's history and culture on your first day? Did you have opportunities to sit down with key managers and employees to learn from their experiences and get a general idea about how each department works?

Each employee needs to know his specific role and how it fits into the overall strategy, have clearly defined KPIs (Key Performance Indicators) and understand the organization's expectations. Training isn't simply showing someone how to perform tasks. Training is walking alongside your employee, modeling the culture, and demonstrating that your work environment is one that encourages learning, allows mistakes, and rewards achievements.

The top places to work know that without proper training, the company will never reach its full potential. Employee retention will be dismal due to poor morale. Without a formal training program a company might be profitable, but long term success will be elusive.

If you don't have a training team or program in place, review your management team's work history files and – fingers crossed - you'll find that you have someone working for you who has experience with training. If no one fits the bill, or if the employee who does is strapped with other priorities, interview three recommended training firms or consultants within thirty days, and hire the one that best fits your culture.

Invest in the highest level of professional your budget allows. If your top pick is too expensive, ask if you can negotiate the fees, set them up on retainer for two or three months, or do half of the training sessions via web conference. Assign one point-person on your team to be the training consultant's primary liaison, with the understanding that everything taught will be documented and incorporated into your in-house training program going forward.

Your formal training program should include:

- Company history
- Your mission, vision and strategy
- The industry and competitive landscape
- How you operate
- Job-specific training
- Expectations for the position
- Onboarding
- The Culture
- Strategic Calendar
- Company Calendar
  - o Customer events
  - o Employee events
  - o Paid holidays
- Helpful Hints
  - o How to use copier, phone, set-up email and voice mail, etc.
  - o Contact information for relevant departments
    - IT/help desk, receptionist, shipping and receiving, department heads

When you invest in your employees, you need to demonstrate trust and be transparent. The manager who fears new hires or isn't transparent shouldn't be in management. If you're afraid to disclose sales goals, or marketing budgets, or invite others to product launch meetings, then there is something seriously amiss.

Something to consider incorporating into your training program is "Lunch with the President." When I was at Robbins Brothers, the new president, Andy, wanted to connect with the teams at the home office and in the stores. He set up a monthly meeting where a department would be treated to lunch in his office and could ask any questions about the company. Anything. Soon we all knew that this was meant as a way to build bridges, and although the new person in charge wasn't a member of the family, it was clear he wanted to continue the culture of transparency that was the reason many employees stayed with the company for 10, 20 and 30 years.

The new president's second year, as fourth quarter approached, an announcement went out that Andy would be setting up an omelet bar and would be making breakfast-to-order on an upcoming Friday. He had the reputation of a gourmet chef who loved to cook, but he certainly surprised us all when we walked out into the hallway to find two tables of ingredients, from avocados to zucchini, and he delighted the home office of 60+ employees by making omelets, to-order, and spending about two hours cooking. The president went on to every store in the chain, from San Diego up to San Fernando Valley, then flew east to Dallas and Houston, doing the same thing for the stores on Saturday or Sunday mornings before they opened. And he did this in November and December, the busiest time of the year for retail.

Imagine if new employees were invited to meet with the CEO their first week? Picture a small group of college grads, seasoned experts and maybe a part-timer sitting around the president's desk, eating Jimmy John's or sharing a pizza, learning about culture and strategy from the person who runs the company? My guess is you'd see employee retention increase and word-of-mouth recruiting take over as the most effective way to find new employees.

Training need not be long and tedious. Most individuals will learn over time and at their own pace. Hands-on training is optimal whenever possible, and simulated environments offer great learning opportunities without interfering with day-to-day operations. If your organization is small and training will have to take place on the floor and in real-time, just be transparent with your customers and let them know you're helping a new hire learn the ropes.

Research training programs at other companies and other industries to find one that fits your organization. Create an online training system that new hires can log in to from home or at the workplace and encourage all managers to review the program every few months to make sure the material is relevant and up-to-date.

The Soulful Welcome: New Employee Onboarding

If you were ever the "new kid" in school, you may have been fortunate enough to have a thoughtful teacher who assigned a partner to help you through the first week. The fellow student would sit next to you in class, show you to the restroom, sit with you at lunch and help you figure out all the ins-and-outs until you felt familiar in this strange new world. More often than not this partner would turn out to be a good buddy, if not your very best friend.

Imagine now if a "work partner" was assigned at your company to help a new employee get acclimated? Adults get nervous in new situations, too, and having a partner introduce you to new co-workers, the intimidating IT department, the managers and department heads and anyone else you needed to know in the office would help alleviate the jitters.

KICK-OFF: THE SOULFUL EXPERIENCE

You're almost ready to deliver a Soulful Experience. But don't jump the gun.

The old saying is true: you've only got one shot to make a good first impression. You may not have a senior executive with decades of industry experience and a proven track record at impressing even the most discerning customer, but you have formed a strong committee of employees passionate about your brand, and you've done all the hard work. Just don't procrastinate. Or worse yet, don't skip this vital step. Set a realistic timeline for getting the word out about your new experience, set the budget and tactics, and then get started.

The sooner you formally kick-off the good news, the sooner your employees can start sharing the news with their social networks, and the sooner you'll see new customers. When you're ready to announce a major change to your company - and culture – I recommend that you kick-off the announcement with an internal event for your employees before doing anything else. You'll have their feedback from the training and prep meetings, and they'll be excited and honored to be at a company that shares news with the staff before anyone else.

This isn't your typical meeting, after all, and making a change this big requires getting out of the conference room or cafeteria. If you're the CEO of a small company, host a party at your home or restaurant. A large staff can be accommodated in a rented-out movie theater, a community center or even a small nightclub with a stage. The space will communicate to the team that things are going to really change, so be sure the venue is unique and suits the message you're going to share.

Pick a theme for the event that supports your new direction. Skip the boring email invite and Powerpoint presentation and share the news in an unexpected way. Print out invitations and put one on every employee's desk or in their mailbox, along with a candy bar or gift card. The goal of the kick-off is to make the new experience relevant to all employees so they in turn will make it relevant to the customers.

At the kick-off event after sharing details about the new focus on providing a Soulful Experience, surprise your employees with some a new perk. Perhaps an extra vacation day this year and every year for everyone's commitment, free breakfast every Friday?

Do whatever it takes for the people on your team to inherently know what your brand represents. Executing the new experience with a concise vision and mission will turn your employees into natural brand ambassadors. Your advertising, store experience and customer service will then radiate from your culture.

If your company hasn't actively participated in community outreach, use the kick-off to let the team know you'll now be partnering with a local charity. And if your CFO and HR leaders approve, go ahead and give each employee eight paid hours a year or every six months to volunteer with the charity.

Soon after your employees have been brought into the loop, make formal announcements about your Soulful Experience to vendors, existing customers, the social and local communities, and the media:

o   Announcement to vendors via email
o   Formal roll-out to customers via email or USPS
o   Store:
  ▪   Exterior banner on building that states "Now Offering The Soulful Experience"
  ▪   Digital message on video wall or TVs
  ▪   Signage as they enter your business
o   Website, Social Media and Digital Ads:
  o   Banner and badge that states "Now Offering The Soulful Experience"

Announcement to Media

- Press Release (also include details about your new community outreach program and how employees will be involved)
- Calls and emails to local business journal, newspapers, radio and TV stations
- Community Events
- Customer (or Vendor) Appreciation Day
- Social Media – this is where your employees step up as ambassadors

Marcus Lemonis, successful entrepreneur, owner/investor of several hundred companies, and host of the popular CNBC show "The Profit" says this about investing in business:

"Yes, it is about making money.
But for me it's largely about how business
can transform people's lives."

Before we wrap up, I want to reiterate the importance of following up with your leaders and employees after you implement the steps learned about in this book.

Four "musts" to take away:

1. Put monthly or quarterly check-ups on the calendar NOW, and send the meeting invitation out to all team leaders and Soulful Experience committee members.
2. Attend committee meetings regularly when your schedule allows, and at the very least have committee chairpersons meet with you to provide updates.
3. Hold people accountable to do the right thing and adhere to your company vision, mission and employee handbook. No one is exempt from doing the right thing. Every executive, manager and employee should be held accountable.
4. Strategy. Strategy. Strategy. Stay on the course, follow the strategic plan and calendars, adapt when necessary, and communicate results.

I also recommend you find trusted leaders outside of the company to be on your advisory board.

Providing a Soulful Experience is doing the right thing for your customers, for your employees, and yes, for your business.

THE SOULFUL EXPERIENCE ASSESSMENT

Does your business provide a Soulful customer experience, or is improvement needed?

Take this quick Soulful Experience assessment:

Rate Your Experience on a Scale of 1-7
(1 – oh-no/poor experience, 7 - "The Soulful Experience")

Initial perception of brand _____
(Website/digital ad, other advertising, reputation)

Exterior appearance & signage _____
(Window displays, parking lot, sidewalk in front of place)

Greeting once inside _____
(How long did it take to be acknowledged?)

Appearance of establishment once inside _____

That extra "something" (beverage, snacks, live musician?) _____

Cleanliness of main area, restrooms, counters, checkout _____

Quality of product and service _____
(Whether socks or sake, candy or chicken cordon bleu)

Employee expertise, confidence and attentiveness   _____

Do you want to be part of this brand's story?   _____

Point of sale   _____
(Wait time, explanation of return policy, warranty, etc.)

Follow-up after the sale   _____
(i.e. personal phone call or email, thank you card)

Total: _____

Score of 70-77:   Soulful Experience
Score of 55-69:   So-so Experience
Score of less than 55:   Oh-no Experience

If you scored in the Soulful Experience range, congrats! Send an email to me at <u>diane@thesoulfulexperience.com</u> and I'll send you a digital badge to place on your website and social pages that will let the world know you provide a Soulful Experience.

RECOMMENDED BOOKS FOR FURTHER BUSINESS INSPIRATION

Brand Storytelling

- Building a Story Brand – Donald Miller
- Emotional Branding – Marc Gobe

Leadership & Culture

- The Rolling Desk - David J. Morris and Chris Heyer
- Startup Leadership - Derek Lidow
- Leadership 101 – What Every Leader Needs to Know – John C. Maxwell
- The Go-Getter - Peter B. Kyne

Building a Business

- Blue Collar Gold - Mark Stoner
- Why Now is the Time to Crush It! – Gary Vaynerchuck

Career and Calling

- A Breathtaking Journey Toward a Life of Meaning - Rebekah Lyons
- You Are Free: Be Who You Already Are – Rebekah Lyons
- God of the Underdogs – Matt Keller

ACKNOWLEDGMENTS

A heartfelt "thank you" to friends and family from all walks of life. This list includes (but is certainly not limited to): Carla and Greg, Tara, Janice, Stephanie, Tracey L., David, Sydney, Ruben, CarolAnne, Dani and Chris, Edie-mom, Elisa, Jamie, Jane, David (and the extended Tharp and Sheer families), Jennie and Frank, Jennifer, Lisa, Kurt and Lori, Misty and Ron, Kelsey, Marchant, Linda, Dylan, Alli, Shulie, Sam H., Mark P., Phil and Teresa, Tracy R. and her tribe, my old RB Team (Newman!), my fab Monrovia neighbors, Bob & Shirley, Jenny L., Jennifer H-B, WJA, family in England and the States, Tiffany, and of course Jen, Kev, Victoria, Noah and Eli.

To Steph, Janice, and the Kitchen Table Fellowship ladies: Psalms will always be "our book." God's timing was certainly perfect when he brought me to your group.

To the Selah Sisters: you know how to celebrate life and I love you so much. Keep the Los Olivos B&B dream alive!

To Linda: You teased me about drinking too much coffee in college as I pulled all-nighters to finish English papers. Fast-forward a few decades and here you are proofreading my little book. From the bottom of my heart, thank you.

To Dave, Lauren, Kristyn, Corey, Diane, Carmen, Laura, Sarah, Brooke, Emma F., Cheryl P.: You are each so precious and a gift from God.

To Danielle, Pastor Doug and the Plum Creek fourth and fifth graders: You reminded me that kindness is as essential in today's crazy world as it was when Jesus taught the disciples to be kind to each other. Even to our enemies.

To Donne and Cindy Kerestic, Steve and Marisa Robbins, Larry Gomperts and other mentors mentioned in this book: your time, generosity, compassion and knowledge have inspired me to mentor others. Thank you for teaching me about business, but more importantly for continuing to "walk the walk" of a true leader who puts family first, gives back to the community, and knows that employees are the most vital part of any company. Should "The Soulful Experience" become a movement, you'll be considered the trailblazers.

And most of all, thank you to my Heavenly Father, to Jesus, and to the Holy Spirit.

Romans 5:2-5 "Through Him we have also obtained access by faith into this grace in which we stand, and we rejoice in hope of the glory of God. More than that, we also rejoice in our sufferings, knowing that suffering produces endurance, and endurance produces character, and character produces hope. And hope does not put us to shame, because God's love has been poured out into our hearts through the Holy Spirit who has been given to us."

Romans 5:8 "God shows His love for us in that while were still sinners, Christ died for us."

1 John 4:7-8 "Beloved, let us love one another, for love is from God, and whoever loves has been born of God and knows God. Anyone who does not love does not know God, because God is love."

VISION AND MISSION NOTES

AREAS WHERE WE CAN IMPROVE

DREAM ORGANIZATIONAL CHART

COMMITTEES AND CHAIRPERSONS

IDEAS TO SHARE WITH TEAM

IDEAS TO SHARE WITH TEAM

CPSIA information can be obtained
at www.ICGtesting.com
Printed in the USA
FFOW03n1407260418
46377229-48076FF

9 781973 623632

QUANTUM WRITER

Write Easily, Less Stress,
Better Results

Bobbi DePorter